A Commentary on the Book of
REVELATION

Copyright © 2008, 2012, 2013 David Pawson

The right of David Pawson to be identified as author of this work
has been asserted by him in accordance with the
Copyright, Designs and Patents Act 1988. All rights reserved.
No part of this publication may be reproduced or transmitted in any form or by any
means, electronic or mechanical, including photocopy, recording or any information
storage and retrieval system,
without prior permission in writing from the publisher.

First published in Great Britain in 2008
under the title "Come with me through Revelation"
by Terra Nova Publications International Ltd.
Reprinted 2012

This edition published in 2013 by
Anchor Recordings Ltd
72 The Street, Kennington, Ashford TN24 9HS UK

For more of David Pawson's teaching,
including MP3s, DVDs and CDs, go to
www.davidpawson.com
For further information, email info@davidpawsonministry.com

Scripture quotations taken from the
HOLY BIBLE, NEW INTERNATIONAL VERSION.
Copyright © 1973, 1978, 1984 by International Bible Society.
Used by permission of Hodder & Stoughton Publishers,
a member of the Hachette Livre UK Group.
All rights reserved.
"NIV" is a registered trademark of International Bible Society.
UK trademark number 1448790.

USA acknowledgement:
Scriptures taken from the Holy Bible, New International Version®, NIV®.
Copyright © 1973, 1978, 1984, 2011 by Biblica, Inc.™
Used by permission of Zondervan.
All rights reserved worldwide.
www.zondervan.com
The "NIV" and "New International Version" are trademarks registered
in the United States Patent and Trademark Office by Biblica, Inc.™

ISBN 978-1-909886-25-4

Contents

PREFACE

This book is based on a series of talks. Originating as it does from the spoken word, its style will be found by many readers to be somewhat different from my usual written style. It is hoped that this will not detract from the substance of the biblical teaching found here.

As always, I ask the reader to compare everything I say or write with what is written in the Bible and, if at any point a conflict is found, always to rely upon the clear teaching of scripture.

David Pawson

INTRODUCTION

The opening verses of Revelation give you the flavour and the majesty of this amazing book. We must clear the ground first, and just as a new site is cleared by bulldozers before the new building goes up I want to prepare the site.

The book of Revelation is the strangest book in the Bible. There are some passages elsewhere that are rather like it — in Daniel, Ezekiel, Mark 13 or Matthew 24 — but this whole book is unique and it is very strange. It is a different book from any of the others, and it is a more difficult book than any of the others, so many people tend to leave it alone. It is one of the books of the Bible most neglected by churchgoers. Readers tend to be a little uneasy with it; they do not feel at home in these rather strange pages. Opinions have varied tremendously about this book — from very low opinions to very high opinions. Here is a selection.

Here are some of the low opinions among human beings. 'As many riddles as there are words', says one person. Another says, 'a farrago of baseless fantasies'. Another calls it 'a haphazard accumulation of weird symbols'. Another said, 'It either finds a man mad or leaves him mad', and even Martin Luther said that, 'it is a pity it ever got into the New Testament', proving that he was no more infallible than the Pope whose infallibility he questioned.

On the high side, here are some other opinions by those who have studied this book. 'The only masterpiece of pure art in the New Testament'. William Barclay's opinion was this: 'It is infinitely worthwhile to wrestle with until it gives its blessing and opens its riches.' Another wrote that it is 'beautiful beyond description'. Who is right in such a mixture of opinions?

Let me now move outside human opinion, from the very lowest opinion of this book to the very highest. The lowest belongs to the devil and the highest belongs to God. Satan has the lowest opinion of anyone in this book and he loathes it. He will try to stop you reading two books in the Bible if he possibly can: Genesis and Revelation. These are the two books about him which tell us what terrible evil he has done and what his doom and destiny are, and he hates you to know that; he hates you to know that one day he will be cast into a bottomless pit. He wants you to give him respect, to honour him, and therefore he will keep you out of this book if he can, and he has a very low opinion of it. No wonder that the result of so many scholars' work has been to put the simple believer off reading Genesis and Revelation, and I am sure the devil was thrilled.

The highest opinion of this book is God's opinion. Do you know what God said about this book, that he says about no other in the whole Bible? First of all he said, *Blessed is the one who reads the words of this prophecy.* At the beginning there is a beatitude pronounced on those who read it aloud in a congregation, so I am going to get a blessing for reading it to my congregation; you will get a blessing if you hear it and take to heart what is written in it.

Then, at the end of the book, God pronounces a curse on anyone who takes a little bit away from this book or adds a little bit to it. It is unique in the annals of scripture for God to have blessed those who read it as it stands, and cursed those who tamper with it, and this should make us read this book with very real interest.

Interpretations vary tremendously — from what I have called the grossly literal to the grotesquely allegorical. It is quite extraordinary how many weird and strange ideas people have got out of this book. Many have therefore got the idea that it is a sealed book, a hidden book, a book for those in the rarefied atmosphere of deep scholarship — not a book for the ordinary man in the street. They could not make a bigger mistake; this book is not a sealed book but a book that is open; it is not a book to hide things from you, it is a book to show things to you; it is not a book that is deliberately obscure, trying to make it difficult for you to see, it is a book that is there to help you to see, and therefore I can only say that I am going to give you my own interpretation, which you must not take as infallible.

The little rhyme that I would urge you to bear in mind constantly as you read is, 'Don't take it from me, but search and see.' And I am only hoping that what I write will encourage you to read it for yourself and not say, 'David Pawson says . . . .' I am no more infallible than Martin Luther, and you must not take my word as the last word. But I will give you what seems to me the straightforward, simple, clear interpretation of this book — if there is such a thing.

The crucial question is: what sort of a book is it? There are six main answers that have been given to this and I have given them various titles. First of all, there are those who say it is an APOCALYPTIC book. Now what do we mean by this word 'apocalyptic'? It describes a certain kind of exciting literature that is usually written in times of terrible trouble. It is often written in symbolic form, so that only those who have got the key to it will understand and therefore there will be no danger attached to reading it. But it is nevertheless meant to help people to see that, however deep the present troubles may be, God is on the throne, right will triumph, and wrong will be conquered; it is an encouraging kind of literature. But the word 'apocalyptic' — which is, incidentally, the very first word in this book, translated in English 'revelation' — or the word 'apocalypse' means a peep behind the scenes. Now that is a lovely word, to go backstage, to see who is pulling the strings, to see who is in charge, to see what is really happening.

I am quite sure that the last time you read the Sunday papers you were depressed. Every week it is churned out — the filth and the hatred and the war and the cruelty of men, and people get troubled by what is happening on the stage of life. This book says come around behind the scenes. Literally, the word means to draw back the curtains, to show you what is happening behind the scenes, to show you who is in control, and therefore apocalyptic literature is very encouraging in dark and dangerous and difficult times, such as we are now living in, because behind the scenes God is on the throne. But it is not just an unveiling of God — a peep behind the scenes at God — it is a revelation of Jesus. In other words, behind the stage of human history, Jesus is in charge. All authority in heaven and on earth are in his hands, and therefore we are going to catch a glimpse of Jesus as King of kings and Lord of lords.

Now there are three things that Jesus is. He is our Prophet, he is our Priest and he is our King. If you study the Gospels you will discover the truth that he is Prophet; if you study the epistles you discover the truth that he is Priest, but it is when you get to this book that you discover that he is King. I have a famous picture that I was given a long time ago — Charles Butler's masterpiece: *King of kings*. In the centre is King

Jesus with a luminous robe depicted in a way that is unlike any other artistic representation. There he is, King of kings, in his simplicity, with a crown of thorns. Behind him, the devil cowers — the defeated prince of this world. Gathered around him are 159 royal people of history, kings and queens, all adopting in the picture the attitude they adopted to Jesus in their lives. Here is Edward the Confessor, holding out his crown to Jesus; here is Napoleon Bonaparte, standing aloof from this King of kings; but all of them are looking at this King. What a picture! Now that is the artist capturing the book of Revelation. It is a revelation of Jesus as King of kings and Lord of lords. This is the thrill of reading it.

There are four things that are revealed about Jesus uniquely in this book. First of all, that when he comes back he will come to judge the quick and the dead. He will come to bring *retribution*. There is coming the greatest day of human history, and this book depicts the wrath of God in that time. We have never seen Jesus like this. Once, when he cleaned out the temple, people caught just a glimpse of the wrath of Jesus, but there is a day coming when everybody will see, and those who have been cruel and those who have been unkind, and those who have been jealous and those who have been bad-tempered, will see his anger against all that men have done. It is said of F W Robertson of Brighton that once, while walking along Brighton seafront, he saw a young man who had blasted the purity of a girl in his church, and he was so angry with that young man that he bit his lip until it bled. One day, Jesus will show his wrath for all that has been done to the children of God. Retribution — this is a peep behind the scenes.

Secondly, we see here a Lord Jesus who is not only coming to bring retribution but also to bring *reward*. Time and again in this book there are promises that those who have overcome will be given a crown of life — Jesus coming to reward those who have served him on earth, those who may never have been noticed by human beings; quietly, in their own way they have served God, they have even died for the faith, and maybe no-one knew that they had died. There are people dying for the faith today, in China and elsewhere, who we do not know about. One day Jesus will be seen rewarding such people. That is another glimpse we have here of Jesus.

Thirdly, here is a glimpse of Jesus *recreating* or renovating the entire universe, making a new heaven and a new earth, putting everything right, starting all over again, and re-making all that went wrong.

Fourthly, most important, we have here a glimpse of Jesus *reigning* for ever and ever. One day he will wear not a crown of thorns but many crowns of royalty. We have never seen that; nobody has ever seen that, except the man who wrote this book, and he saw it in a vision of the future, but one day we shall sing 'crown him with many crowns' because we will be able to see it before our very eyes.

We can sum up the theme of Revelation in 17:14 thus: *They will make war against the Lamb, but the Lamb will overcome them because he is Lord of lords and King of kings — and with him will be his called, chosen and faithful followers.*

Now that is why we call it an apocalyptic book, an unveiling of the future.

Now the second question: who was the author who wrote this book? It is an ECSTATIC book. Let me tell you what I mean by that. It comes from the actual pen of John, the beloved apostle, now the aged apostle. Let us look at this man. First of all, where is he? I was interested to come across a photograph of a Greek island called Patmos, in the Aegean Sea, and that is where the aged 'beloved apostle' was when he wrote this book. It came from his hand; his body was there. Now, it looks a lovely island. But in fact he was in prison in chains. This was the equivalent of Siberia in the ancient world; this was where criminals were banished and kept away so that they could not pollute society and poison other people. If you look at a map of the Aegean Sea, and what is now the western end of Turkey, you can see Greece, and the Bosphorus leading through to the Black Sea. Right in the middle of the Aegean is the island of Patmos. John had been travelling freely around a group of seven churches on the mainland — what we now call Turkey and which was then called Asia. His body was there, but if that was all we could say about John this book would never have been written. If his body was in the prison, where was his mind? His mind was in the scriptures. Do you realise that out of 404 verses there are 400 allusions to the Old Testament? Here was a man who was steeped in his Bible, and that was where his mind was. He quotes the Bible as often as he writes a sentence in this, packing in the scriptures. Twenty-four out of thirty-nine books in the Old Testament are referred to in this one book of Revelation.

Where was his heart? It was about 150 miles away, for his heart was in that group of churches. As a pastor, his heart is going out to the people he has left. His body is in prison on the island of Patmos; his mind is in the Bible; his heart is in the churches — but where is his spirit? The answer is the spirit is not chained, it is not in prison, his spirit is not in the churches, his spirit is not in the Bible — where is he? The answer is he is in the Spirit on the Lord's Day. His spirit is 'in the Spirit' and can therefore leave his body. The spirit can leave the body even on earth, and to some God has granted that rare privilege so that while the body may be chained the spirit can move and explore God's universe, heaven and earth. I have occasionally known people who have had this experience and who, in the Spirit, were able to move right out into God's whole future —to move out of the present into things yet to come, and to experience things of which they may scarcely speak.

But when we have said all that, John was not the author of the book. We are told that he was given this book by an angel, and that means a heavenly messenger. If you do not believe in angels you are going to have problems with this book. We bump into an increasing number of them until they crowd the pages more than human beings. All people will believe in angels one day, because they will see them. Here they are, striding through these pages as God's messengers. Did an angel write this book? No. Who gave the angel the message? The answer is Jesus Christ, for the phrase *revelation of Jesus* not only means something *about* him but something *from* him. Jesus gave it to the angel who gave it to John. Did Jesus write this book? No. The answer is, at the very beginning, that God gave it to Jesus, who gave it to the angel, who gave it to John, and John gave it to us —and I am giving it to you. Here is the series of links in the heavenly chain of Revelation. This is God's book, and as we read it I want you to remember that this is not some human flight of fantasy, this is not some human opinion about what is going to happen in the future, this is what God says. Therefore, there is no discussion, there can be no argument, there can only be a 'lost in wonder, love and praise' attitude towards this. You can either accept it or you can reject it. If you reject it you will one day discover that you were wrong, that you cannot play around with God's

Word. God wrote it. It is an ecstatic book in which, in a deep experience of his spirit leaving his body, John was able to be given a message that no other man could possibly have given us because nobody knows the future.

Next, Revelation is a SYMBOLIC book. This raises the question: how does one interpret the signs? It is full of weird and wonderful signs — figures of speech, numerical figures, and so on. Some people take it all quite literally, some people take it allegorically, a bit like *The Pilgrim's Progress*, and I think the truth probably lies in between. Let me give you the four approaches that I take in trying to unravel the symbols. We are not used to talking in symbols today. Let me put it like this: suppose that I am driving along the road and I come to a sign which says 'school' and there is a little picture of a silhouette of a ten-year-old girl and a six-year-old boy, as far as I can judge from the roadside, running across the road. Does that sign mean that very shortly I will see a ten-year-old girl and a six-year-old boy running across the road? No. It is a sign. It would be wrong to press it literally, but I must take it as pointing to reality and I can expect to see children running across the road. A sign is something that points to reality beyond itself. It corresponds to that reality, it tells you about that reality, but you cannot press it too far literally. This book is full of signposts like that, symbolic signs, so that if you see a sign for a level crossing it may not look quite like the sign, but the sign has told you what to expect. That is the book of Revelation, and if you approach the signs like that then it seems to me you have no difficulty in interpreting them.

Some, of course, are quite *obvious*: the lake of fire, the books that are open, the great white throne; the meaning of those signs is perfectly obvious and nobody argues.

Some of the signs are *explained*: the seven stars; the seven lampstands; the seven lamps; incense, which refers to prayer; the dragon, which stands for the devil. You do not expect to see a dragon when this book talks about a dragon, but it is a clear symbol of the devil.

Some signs are paralleled elsewhere in the Bible — the tree of life, manna, the rod of iron, the morning star, the four horsemen, the four beasts; all you need to do with those is to look up the rest of the Bible and see what they mean.

There are also some *obscure* signs, and when we come to them I will be quite frank and tell you that I cannot make much of them either. I have put among the obscure signs the white stone; and the two witnesses I think are a debatable sign, the wine press also, but things like that we shall tackle as we come to them. There are not many that are obscure, and the secret is to work from the whole to the parts, from the general to the particular and when you come to a thing that you do not understand, to ask about the general setting in which it is, and see if that helps.

Having said all that, I would like to conclude this section by pointing out first that there is one key that we do not possess to open this book: most of us do not suffer persecution. When you suffer for the faith you will understand this book better. It was written for those who are going through it. It is very interesting that Chinese Christians have been devouring this book for some time. They have the key that unlocks the meaning; they are suffering for their faith. They have come to the beast whose number is 666 — there is a funny number and a symbol, but in the Chinese People's Government in Beijing there were 666 representatives. Those Christians read this book and they had no problem in seeing the Antichrist working through a totalitarian government. You have to suffer if you are going to understand this book. Maybe we will yet have that key in the West, and if we do it will have been very helpful that we have been through this book first. There is another key that we do have and that is the spirit of prophecy — and that spirit of prophecy enabled the book to be written, and will enable us to read it.

Revelation is also an HISTORIC book. What is its background? What was happening about the time it was written? We do not know for certain when it was written, but it was either in the middle of the first century, in the time of Nero, or in the time of the emperor Domitian. I plump for the latter. All the pointers seem to point that way, towards the end of the first century. What was happening? Politically it was a period of unparalleled power. The emperors had risen in power, until now the emperor called himself god and ruled the world. It was similar to what Mao Tse-tung did in China. It was that kind of situation — a police state. Vespasian had conquered the Dutch and Gauls and subdued them completely; Titus had subdued the Jews; Domitian subdued the British and the Germans, and now the whole world was under the thumb of one man who claimed to be divine. This was the political background. Against this background there was peace — he ensured that there was. There was prosperity, and since people want peace and prosperity more than anything else, then they would accept a dictator who would give them both, and Domitian did, at a price, and the price was liberty of conscience. I predict on the basis of the book of Revelation that one day the whole world will be so anxious to have peace and prosperity that they will allow one man to dictate, because he will give it to them, at the price of liberty of conscience.

That is the political background. As to the social background, the world was developing culture and commerce and there was corruption. In religion there was a world movement, an ecumenical movement, combining all gods and all religions, and I predict on the basis of the book of Revelation that this is the next big development in world history today — there will be an ecumenical movement between the different religions of the world. That was what was happening then. The Roman emperor had built the Pantheon, with its niches for every little god, so you could mix all the religions and unite the world religiously. The Christians would not join in. There is only one God and they would not bow down and say, 'Caesar is Lord', 'Caesar is God', nor would they put Jesus alongside the other gods, even though they were offered a place. It is against this background of totalitarianism, a background of state control, even of religion, that this book was written — and no wonder it was needed. There were people who were saying, 'Where is God?'; 'Who is in charge of the world?' With all this going on, it looks as if Domitian can get away with anything. He can call himself god and nobody pushes him off that throne. There were Christians in China who felt that way about Mao. There have been Christians in Cuba who have felt that way about Fidel Castro; there are Christians all over the world who ask: 'Where is God? What is he doing?' These men are getting away with it, and they are controlling everything, and they are stamping out the Christian faith. But the book of Revelation says come behind the curtains, come behind the scenes, and you will see what is going to happen to world powers. This book is a theology of power. We live in the age of power — power blocs, military power — and I want to quote from Psalm 62,

One thing God has spoken,
two things have I heard:
that you, O God, are strong . . . .

That is what this book is all about: the strength or power of God. Power does not belong to presidents and prime ministers, power belongs to God. That is where real power resides, and when you have read this book you will see it.

It is a PROPHETIC book. It is a book about the future. Prophets speak about the future, they predict what is going to happen. I want to give you now the four main fulfilments, or the four main theories, about interpreting this book.

The problem is this. The first few chapters really reflect the days in which John lived 2000 years ago — churches such as those at Thyatira, Ephesus, and so on. The last two chapters of this book clearly refer to the end of history. The big question, therefore, is: to what part of history do chapters 4 – 20 refer? That is the big issue on which interpretations divide. There are four answers.

The *preterist* approach says that these chapters refer to the history at the end of the first century AD and to nothing more, and therefore they really do not concern us at all, they are about history in the first century. Chapters 4 – 20 refer to the past and are not concerned with today.

Secondly, the *historicist* says no, those chapters cover the whole of history, from Christ's first coming to his Second Coming, in chronological calendar order, and therefore you probably reach the Middle Ages by about chapter 12, and then the Reformation by about chapter 14, and so on, and those who take the historicist view usually get to about chapter 19 in their own day. They have been doing this for about 1,000 years already, and one of the problems I have with this view is that no two scholars have ever agreed on which part of history each chapter refers to. I hope I am not caricaturing, but you will gather that I am not going to give you a lot of that point of view. I do not believe that chapters 14–20 are a detailed blueprint of the last 2000 years, and if they were they would cover African, Indian and Chinese history, which most of the people who take that view seem to forget.

Thirdly, the *futurist* takes the view that chapters 4–20 refer to the end of human history. They are still future, all those chapters. We can learn from them what to expect and how to recognise things when they come — but they do not refer to our day, but to the future.

Finally, there is the *idealist* view which is that chapters 4–20 are not about any of these three — past, present or future — but are about principles, ideas, ideals on which God operates in every age, and therefore they do not have any timescale. You take your choice. The line I will be taking is this: I believe that chapters 4–20, taken in their simplest and clearest meaning, refer largely to the future of history, to the end time, to what we may expect before the Second Coming of our Lord. I will still bring in part of the others, because I think the preterist is right in that these chapters were written in that situation long ago, which helps us to understand them. I think the historicist is right in that you can see the foreshadowings of these things right through the last 2,000 years. And I think the idealist is right in that these chapters reveal God's eternal principles. But I am going to rely most heavily on the futurist, because I think that is the most straightforward and the most helpful and the most true to the Bible. I just want you to be aware that there are other views than the one I shall be giving you.

Revelation is a BEATIFIC book. What does that word mean? It means it is a book full of blessing. There are seven beatitudes in this book. 'Beatitudes' (sentences that begin *Blessed are*) describe 'beautiful attitudes', which God blesses. There are three virtues in the Christian life that every one of us needs: *faith*, *hope* and *love*, and the most neglected of these three is *hope*. The greatest of these is love, but the most neglected is hope. And the reason why it is neglected is this: this book, of all the books in the Bible, is given to you to develop your hope, which is that faculty we have for grasping the future and saying the future belongs to Jesus, not to anyone else. I have written down blessings that you will have when you read this book — ten reasons for studying it; ten necessary parts of the Christian life.

1. To know this book is to have a defence against deception. There will be Jehovah's Witnesses and others knocking at your door. They will use this book; you have no right to criticise them unless you know it better than they do. They will use it in a distorted way, you must use it in a true way, and it is a defence against the distortions of sects that are spreading over the world. That is one good reason.

2. To read this book is a preparation for persecution. I do not know if this will happen this decade, but I am absolutely convinced that there is coming a day when in Britain it will be a costly thing to be a Christian, when people will lose their jobs because they are Christians, when people will be alone because they are Christians. I can see that coming, the pointers are all that way. I would just like to add that while humanly speaking I shrink from it, with part of me I hope it will come quickly. I believe that nothing else would draw Christians together more quickly, or set the church on fire, or get rid of the

dross in the body of Christ. If and when that comes, a reading of this book will have got you ready; there is nothing like this to put cast iron into your soul. Jesus said, *'In this world you will have trouble. But take heart! I have overcome the world'* (John 16:33b). How do we know he has? By reading the book of Revelation.

3. This book is a tremendous stimulus to worship. There is more singing in this book than in any book in the New Testament — it is full of song. All Christians will be in the choir in heaven, we will all have good voices. Does that not make you want to shout 'hallelujah'? Of course it does. It is full of worship, full of praise, full of song, new music. We shall be full of praise. People are stimulated to praise God by reading this book. There are eleven major songs in it. Many of our hymns come out of this book, some of them very well known, such as: *Crown him with many crowns, the Lamb upon his throne*.

4. It is an antidote to worldliness. One of the most pressing temptations upon all of us today is this: we are getting earthbound. Even the church is falling into this trap, so that you hardly hear a sermon on heaven or a hymn about heaven. The church is becoming enmeshed in social and political questions. The book of Revelation is needed to get us out of that. I know that the world jibes at us and says, 'pie in the sky when you die' and says, 'you are other-worldly', and, 'you are living in the great beyond, we have got to live here'. Let the world say such things. I say you have to live in that world beyond, you have to get ready for it, and we are the only people who are helping you. Let us get a true perspective, and let us not become this-worldly to the exclusion of the other world. That is not to say that the Christian does not have social and political

responsibilities; we do, but it is to say that if that is someone's main bearing in life then he has got 'off course'. We are called to be pilgrims, not just to help people through this world but to prepare them for the next, which is a far larger calling and a far more important thing. If we do not do it there is no other person who will do it. That is what the church is for, to tell people there is another world and you must be ready for it. The book of Revelation keeps us fixed on a city whose builder and maker is God — like Abraham of old, we become pilgrims; we do not settle for a bungalow on the ground, we look beyond, we look for what God is going to build.

5. This book is an incentive to godliness. Seeing that all these things are to be dissolved, what sort of persons ought we to be? Living our lives in *all godliness and holiness* (1 Timothy 2:2b). If we really realise the world is passing away, what kind of people will we be? The answer is that we will be the sort of people who are going to live in the next world. But if we believe that the world is passing away and that there is nothing beyond, then what sort of people will we be? We would be the sort of people who go out and get drunk every night, having a merry time while we can. But there is going to be a new heaven and a new earth, so what sort of people will you be? This book helps you to be godly. The letters to the seven churches alone will search out your heart until you see yourself as you really are.

6. What a motive for evangelism! If you doubt whether hell is real, if you doubt whether heaven is real, read the book of Revelation. As one scholar has put it, 'Revelation, beyond all other books, has made people feel that heaven is real.' When you get into this, you want to get out and say to everybody, 'This is coming, it is more real than the place in which you

live now, and I want you to be there when it comes.'

7. It is an interpretation of history. It is amazing that pundits in our papers tell us what they think is happening in history, the trends, the directions, what is going to come next; they think they know, and they are like the blind leading the blind. Nobody knows, except the Christian, what history is really unfolding, and where it is really heading, and what is really happening.

Quite simply, at the moment the biggest fact in history is that Satan is seeking to isolate the church from the world. This is the real meaning behind much racial tension and violence. Satan wants to separate different ethnic groups so that no longer can the gospel be spread. Why is China officially closed to missionaries? Why is country after country closing to missionaries? The answer is that Satan is trying to stop the gospel. Every time you open your newspapers and read of race riots here, and closed countries there, you are reading about Satan's activity in his fight against God. This book will help you to read your newspaper with astonishing insight. There will be times when, having studied the book of Revelation, you will pick up your daily paper on Monday morning and say, 'This was what I was learning about in the Bible.' It is an astonishing thing — an interpretation of history.

8. It is an assurance of the outcome of the battle. Somebody in Guildford asked me, after discovering that I was the minister of a church, 'What does it feel like to belong to a dying organisation?' I said, 'I wouldn't know!' I know that the figures are bad, and I know that things look depressing and humanly speaking as we approach the second decade of the twenty-first century and we see how tough it is going to be for churches and Christians — and it is going to be far more

difficult than the past decades — there are those who would become depressed, but do you think I am down-hearted? Never. Why not? Because I have read the book of Revelation and I know what is going to happen. In the battle between the church and the world, or rather the battle between Christ and Satan, who is going to win? No question about that. People talk to me as if man is going to end history by pressing the wrong button. I am not afraid of that because it is not going to happen — God will not let it happen, that is not the way he has planned to end history, and it will not end that way. Is it not wonderful to be in the twenty-first century with that hope? I know the outcome of the battle: God is still on the throne, and history is always in his hands, and the church of Jesus Christ will survive until people of all tribes and kindreds and tongues — a multitude that no man can number — are gathered in.

9. Revelation gives me an understanding of Christ. From time to time people say to me, 'I just believe in Jesus. There are a lot of things you say as a preacher that I don't agree with, but I just believe in Jesus.' Sometimes I talk to people like that and I find they do not believe in *all* of Jesus. They often dismiss whole parts of the Old Testament, though Jesus accepted them. But more than that, they never read the book of Revelation because they do not like the Jesus in it. But if you are going to have the whole picture you must have the whole of Jesus. It is no good saying, 'I like this bit, but not that.' If you are going to believe in Christ and understand him, you have to look at all of him. I know that he came peacefully into Jerusalem on an ass when he was on earth the first time, but I know also that when he comes a second time he will come on a white charger of war, a horse, and that is part of Jesus, and we must have a whole picture of him or you will finish up with a flabby,

27

sentimental portrait that does not correspond to the Jesus you are going to meet.

So we have to understand that Jesus is not 'gentle Jesus, meek and mild'; you will not find that phrase in the Bible, and it is a pity that Charles Wesley ever put it into a hymn — it proved that he was not infallible either, with all his lovely hymns. But in this book Jesus comes as a Lion, not as a Lamb but as the Ram, who is also a Lion, the Lion of the tribe of Judah — and if you are going to have a full view of Jesus you must see Jesus the Lion. Do not stay with that Sunday school picture you had of gentle Jesus meek and mild, see Jesus as the Lion who is to break the seals of history and release his wrath on the affairs of godless men.

10. The blessing of reading this book is that it brings the story of God's redemption to a happy conclusion. It is the completion of the Bible. Without this, the Bible leaves you in mid-air, like the man who read right through a thrilling detective novel and found somebody had torn out the last page, and so was terribly frustrated. In this purposeless world, in this meaningless existence of thousands of our fellow countrymen, this is being expressed in novels, plays and films which have no real ending. Are you getting frustrated with modern plays and novels that just leave you dangling with no ending, nothing that ties up the loose ends? Why is there such a spate of meaningless stories today? It is because life is meaningless to so many and it corresponds to their experience; they enjoy watching them because they say: 'That is me, my story has no ending; my life has no meaning or purpose.'

We know better. It is only in a 'Christian' society that novels end properly and stories come to a conclusion, because only there do you get meaning and purpose. In the great story of the Bible, which began in a garden, it ends in a garden city. It begins with a tree of life being shut off from men, and it ends with a tree of life being available to men again, and if you read the first three chapters and the last three chapters of the Bible you will discover that there is a wonderful correspondence, and there is one thing that could be said of this book: they lived happily ever after. I do not care if a human novel does say that, it cannot ever be true, at the human level. One novel had a lovely misprint and read: '. . . they got married and lived happily even after'! I think that is truer to human existence. There is only one book that can finish up by saying 'and they lived happily ever after' —and that can only be said of those whom God has redeemed and loosed from their sins by the blood of Jesus.

This then is the book of Revelation. I will guarantee that after studying this book you cannot ever be the same again. This book is to be read aloud, listened to, and kept, and those who do so will be blessed.

THE SURPRISING CHRIST
Revelation 1

Come with me in your imagination to a little island in the Dodecanese islands off Turkey, an island about eight miles long and four miles wide shaped rather like a crescent moon. As you look down on that island and see the waves crashing against the rocky cliffs, you will notice that round the bottom of the cliffs are holes, caves in the cliff. These are mines, and working in these mines are political prisoners, and by the mouth of those caves you can see the rough stone houses in which they lived. It is very early morning, the sun has hardly risen, but through the morning mist you can hear the clank of chains as prisoners turn in their sleep. But there is one man lying awake very early, his name John, and he is thinking about the seven churches he cannot go to, for he has been a preacher and a pastor travelling around seven little churches about 150 miles from where he lies. He is going to give those churches a better message than he has ever given them before. He will not be able to give it by word of mouth, he must write it in a letter, but before this day is out he is going to begin the most amazing letter to his seven churches that he has ever written. If he had not written that letter we would not have the book of Revelation, because it is in the form of a letter, it is addressed to those churches, and it has a greeting right at the beginning.

If you had been a Greek writing a letter your first word would have been *grace*, which literally meant 'good luck; may the favour of the gods be upon you.' If you were a Hebrew writing a letter you would have started with the word 'peace', which means harmony — may you have harmony with yourself, with your neighbours, with your enemies, with your God. But when a Christian begins a letter he writes, *grace and peace to you.* It is not a hollow wish, as so much is. I cringe when somebody says, 'The best of luck' — I think, 'What a hollow thing to say.' Even the word *goodbye* is the shortened form of 'God be with ye', but now people just say 'goodbye'. It has lost its meaning. Why? Because just saying the word does not help God to be with someone. Only the Christian can say with certainty: 'Grace and peace to you.' That is the beginning of verse 4. Now why can a Christian say that without saying, 'I hope you'll have grace and peace'? How can a Christian be so sure of 'grace and peace' to you? The answer is: Father, Son and Spirit will give it to you. If I know the Father, Son and Spirit, and you know the Father, Son and Spirit, then I can say, 'Grace and peace to you.' At the end of a service I would never say, 'I hope that you will have the grace of our Lord Jesus and I hope that you will find the love of God, and I wish that you might have the fellowship of the Spirit', I would say, 'The grace of our Lord Jesus be with you, the love of God be with you, the fellowship of the Spirit be with you.' There would be no wishing you good luck; I can say something definite: Grace and peace to you from him who is and who was and who is to be. That is why I can pronounce the Benediction. I am quite sure of God — he always was, he is now, he always will be, so I can say to you 'grace and peace' and every word speaks to us.

We would speak, in modern English, about the seven-fold Spirit of God. In our hymns we speak about the seven-fold, referring to the seven things that Isaiah says the Spirit can give us. John, in his language, would say the seven spirits, not meaning separate spirits, but the seven-fold Spirit. So you have: *Grace and peace to you from him who is, and who was, and who is to come* [that is God the Father], *and from the seven spirits* [or seven-fold Spirit] *before his throne*, [the Holy Spirit] *and from Jesus Christ* . . . — and three things are said about Jesus: (1) He is reliable, he always tells the truth; (2) he has been raised from the dead; and (3) he reigns over all the kings of the earth. That is why you can have grace and peace. The world cannot find peace; they are desperate for it, but they cannot have it because the world does not know the God who always is; the world does not know the seven-fold Spirit of God, and does not trust in Jesus, this reliable, reigning Saviour.

John tells his readers he gives you grace and peace, and there is something you can give back to him — give glory and dominion; tell him what you think of him, he loves to hear. It has been said that in our prayers we are concerned primarily with our needs, in our thanksgiving we are concerned primarily with our blessings, but in worship we are concerned primarily with God himself to the exclusion of all else. The most unselfish thing that you could ever do would be to worship God, not because of what you want from him, not because of what you get from him. I have said this often, but I will never tire of saying it because it is so important: when we come to the time of worship I do not care if the congregation does not get a thing out of it — that is not what it is for — it is so that God can get something out of it. We are there to worship; we are not there to bless ourselves, we are there to bless him, to give him glory and dominion, whether he gives us anything or not. Let us give him glory and dominion.

Let me give you some reasons why you should praise and worship him like this: firstly, for what he has done in the past; and, secondly, for what he is going to do, and it is centred in Jesus. Think of what he has done. Here are three things from verses 5 and 6. First, he loves you. Sometimes somebody has sadly said to me, 'Nobody loves me' — but they are wrong, one person does. Nobody need ever feel that they are unloved if they believe in Jesus: he loves, and he loves us to the end, and there is no end. John the 'beloved disciple' knew this. Would you not want to praise somebody who loved you? They would love to hear you say that they love you and that you love them. So Jesus, as with any human being, loves to hear you say 'I love you' to him who loves us.

The second thing is that he has loosed us, and that means broken the chains that bind us. Think of this: the very wrist of the man who is writing this is clanking as he writes, and he is in prison because of Jesus, and he is chained to the wall because of Jesus, and he writes of Jesus who *has freed us* (1:5) —the irony of it in a sense, and yet the wonder of it. Why does he write these words? Because there are far worse things than physical iron chains to be loosed from. The evil habits of our character are far worse chains than any which men have forged; the chains of our own sin, which we have padlocked, are far worse to him who has loosed us. May I ask you to make a mental list now: from what has Jesus loosed you? Be quite practical about this. You do not have a testimony unless you can say something. Be utterly down to earth. One person I know would say to me, 'he has loosed me from nail biting'. From what has Jesus loosed you, set you free? If he has loosed you from anything, then you will praise him.

Thirdly, he has lifted us after he has loosed us. He loves us, he has loosed us and he has lifted us. Do you realise that if you are a Christian he has placed you in his kingdom and you are now a member of the 'royal family'? That is an amazing privilege, and it should lead you to praise God.

There was a young man in Scotland who sent his Scottish fiancée a prepaid telegram that said, 'Will you marry me?' When she found out that there were twenty-seven free words on a prepaid telegram she said: 'Certainly, willingly, absolutely, eagerly, lovingly, longingly' — and she went right through and used all the words. One word would have done for all those, the word *amen*. It means all those rolled into one; it means: absolutely, certainly, definitely, assuredly, surely — every definite word you can find in the vocabulary, put it into one and spell it in four letters: 'amen'. If you had been in an ancient Hebrew assembly, and somebody said something you agreed with and were sure about, you would have said 'amen' instead of 'hear, hear.' If you had been in a Greek assembly, and a Greek speaker had said something you agreed with, you would have said 'even so'. Now look at the next verse, the end of 1:7 — *So shall it be! Amen.* In other words, it does not matter whether you are Greek, a Hebrew, or anyone else, you can be absolutely sure of some things. First, you can be sure of what Jesus has done for you in the past. He has loved you, he has loosed you, he has lifted you — you can be sure of that, amen. Secondly, you can be absolutely sure of what Jesus is going to do in the future. *So shall it be! Amen.* What is he going to do in the future? He is going to come back to earth. His Second Coming is going to be completely different from the first one. First of all, he is coming with clouds of glory. I remember the first time I flew above the clouds. Have you ever had this experience? Passing through the billowy, cumulus clouds with the sun streaming down on a world that seems full of glory. There is nothing like the clouds from above, especially if you have taken off from a typical English day, with overcast sky and drizzle, and you climb up and come out above those clouds. Isn't it wonderful? There is nothing like the clouds to give you a picture of God's glory. Look up and thank God for clouds. I once lived in a place where we hardly ever saw any, so be thankful for the clouds, they are wonderful and always changing, and always billowing up to heaven.

I remember standing on the Mount of Olives one morning by myself, and looking up. It was a clear blue sky except immediately above the Mount of Olives there was a great bank of clouds, almost too bright to look at, and I thought of this text — *he is coming with the clouds.* Glory — we still talk about trailing clouds of glory, but when he came the first time there were no clouds of glory, it was at night not the daytime, and most people did not notice that he had come — only a handful of people knew. Next time, not only will there be divine glory but there will be human grief because everybody will see him. Can you imagine how they will feel?

Did you ever read as a child that fairy tale about an emperor who visited one of the towns in his kingdom disguised as a beggar? The whole town was waiting for the emperor to come, and this beggar came walking down the road, and they pushed him to the back, saying, 'Out of the way, there is somebody important coming.' Then, the next day, he came in his carriage. They all strained forward eagerly to see who was coming, and they saw the face of the beggar they had pushed around the previous day, and they all felt terrible. It is only a fairy tale, but there will come a day when the whole world will feel like that. This Jesus whom they laughed at, because they laughed at his followers who believed he was alive, this Jesus they ignored, this Jesus they heard about and rejected — they will see him one day. The soldiers who banged the nails through his wrists will see him, and Pilate who washed his hands of him will see him, those who pierced him will see him. It is awful seeing someone that you have done something to without realising. The horror of it! I remember once seeing a father looking at a child who was horribly deformed because of something the father had done without realising, without thinking, and I remember the look on that father's face as he saw what he had done to the child. This will be nothing compared with what the world will feel when they see Jesus — divine glory and human grief will be combined — *So shall it be! Amen.* There will be no geographical limit, no historical limit, every eye will see him, and all the tribes of the earth will be sorry that they turned this man down who was the Son of God.

Why is John so sure about the future? Why is he so certain that all this will happen? The answer is that he is absolutely sure of God. If you are sure of God you will be sure of the future. There are two things about God that he is sure of. First of all, God is the 'A–Z'. In other words, before anything else was, there was God; after everything else has gone, there is God. God was there at the beginning, God will be there at the end; God is, and was, and is to come. God is always there, therefore you can be sure of the future.

Secondly, God is not only permanent, he is powerful, he is the Almighty. The one thing that keeps me going when I read the newspapers and watch the news reports of the disasters and the destruction around the world is this: God is Almighty and nobody can stop him doing what he wants to do.

Now we come to the main part of this chapter's study: verses 9–20, the vision that John had. It began with something he heard: a voice. We notice where he heard it: he was in prison. We notice when he heard it: on the 'Lord's Day'. We notice how he heard it: *in the Spirit.* That phrase has been used far

37

too freely. It is spelt with a capital *s*. It does not mean to be in the right mood on Sunday. To be *in the Spirit* is to be supernaturally controlled in your faculties, and alas that is not a common experience today. It is an experience we have watered down and used as a term for being in a kind of reverent mood on Sunday morning. But to be *in the Spirit* means that your eyes see things that otherwise they never would see, that your ears hear voices that otherwise you would never hear, that your mouth says things that otherwise you would never have said — that is what it is to be in the Spirit, and it is a wonderful experience. John had this experience on this particular morning — maybe he did not have it often, but here in a jail he is in the Spirit and he dreamed dreams, and he saw visions, and he heard voices — supernatural voices, supernatural visions.

The first thing he heard was this voice. I would first like to point out the utter humility of verse 9. He could have said, 'I, John, your father in God who am suffering more than any of you for the gospel', and it would have been true, but instead he says, even though he is an older, wiser saint, *'I, John, your brother'*, even though he is suffering worse than any of them. That is a humble mind with a humble man behind it, putting himself on the same level as simple Christians — what a lovely approach.

Now the voice was *like a trumpet*. It is the one instrument that makes us think of the future. It is piercing, it is commanding, it is penetrating, it makes you listen and pay attention. There is going to be a day — the noisiest day in the world's history — when the trumpet shall sound, the archangel will cry out with a shouted command; and the word *trumpet* occurs more in the last book in the Bible than anywhere else in the New Testament. It is quite frequent in the Old, but this is the book of trumpets, and though most people associate harps with heaven, I associate trumpets. It was a voice like a trumpet: piercing, loud, penetrating.

Because John was in the Spirit when he heard it, not another prisoner in the cell woke up. This is what it is to be *in the Spirit*, to be secretly in tune with something that others do not hear. A long time ago, in church, we were broadcasting a morning service through the BBC. Somebody some distance away wanted to listen but was on duty as a steward in their church, where they worked. So he got a small radio with a little earphone, and he went to his own service, but all the time he was standing with a hymn book in his hand he was listening in to me at Gold Hill Baptist Church. Even while he was taking the collection he was still listening in to our service. It is a silly illustration, but when you are in the Spirit you could be alone in a congregation, hearing something, seeing something, having a direct revelation from God. If you do, you will discover that the church has gone, that nobody else is around, you are just alone with God. I pray that you will have such experiences from time to time, as the Lord sees that you need them and sees that you could be blessed by one. So John heard a trumpet and nobody else heard a thing; he was in the Spirit on the Lord's Day and was on a different wavelength, and was now hearing things that were there all the time but other people could not hear them. In church there is music, all kinds of music filling the place; you cannot hear it because you are not on the wavelength, you are not on the frequency, but it is there, it is in the room, music being broadcast, and if we had a receiver we could hear it. God does not need radios — a person who is in the Spirit can hear and see things nobody else can hear and see.

So John turned to *see the voice* — that is an extraordinary phrase — and at first he only saw some lampstands; candlestick kind of things, seven of them standing; and then he saw some stars — and then he gasped because he saw a person standing. Now, I hope, sincerely, that you are not going to be disturbed or disappointed by the next few verses. All of us have a picture of Jesus as we like to think of him, usually built upon Sunday school pictures that we saw when we were young. Think of the usual pictures that you see of him, with blond hair and blue eyes. He does not look like that at all, not now. He may have looked like that once, I do not know. He may have been dark, he may have been fair (he was probably dark); but his hair is not that colour, it is neither fair nor dark, not now. The important thing is that Christians should know what Jesus looks like now. Sometimes parents cling to a photograph of their little child as a baby after the child has grown up, with an almost subconscious wish that the child was still a little baby, but you have got to live with people as they are now if the relationship is going to be real; you cannot live with a picture, you must live with a person. And it is terribly important that Christians should grow up and live with Jesus as he is now, not with a kind of sentimental picture of a fair-haired person with blue eyes, such as you have seen in Sunday school take home papers, otherwise you will get a distorted view. It is very healthy for you to read frequently verses 12–16.

What does he look like now? Certainly, he still looks human. He has the shape and features of a human being. He is like a Son of Man. He looks human and yet he looks divine as well. His clothes are down to his feet. The last time the public saw him he was naked on the cross. Now we are not to think of him like that, but with robes to his feet. Secondly, his hair is as white as snow. Jesus is white-haired now. I have never yet seen a picture of Jesus in any church or Sunday school or book or art gallery that painted him as he looks now, white-haired. Why is he white-haired? Because he is the Ancient of Days. He is centuries old; he has been from all time and his hair is pure white.

Thirdly, his eyes are blazing, x-ray eyes — no wonder at his trial they blindfolded him; those eyes looked you right through, x-ray eyes blazing with anger, when necessary. People feared his eyes even during his life, what it will be like when he comes again I do not know. Burnished feet that look as if they are in metal. Why? These are feet that can trample. His voice is a booming voice — it drowns all others. Now bear in mind that John was lying near the shore of an island in the Aegean sea, and the breakers crashed on the rocks — that is the nearest sound on earth to the voice of Jesus now, like the sound of crashing waves. His mouth, or rather his tongue, is like a bayonet, and interestingly enough the Roman short sword used for attack was exactly the shape of a human tongue. It is saying that his tongue is his weapon — it always was. When Jesus attacked people it was with his tongue — '*you hypocrites! You are like whitewashed tombs*' — he needs no other weapon but his tongue, his word strips the excuses away. And his face. If you have ever tried to look directly at the sun at midday, then you have got the nearest thing you will know on earth to the face of Jesus now. Can you see that picture? The reaction of this man: he fell down in a faint, he became *as though dead*. Well, if the beloved apostle had that reaction, what will the world think when they see a Jesus like that? Treating him as a sentimental Sunday school figure that we can dismiss when we become adults does us no good. What will men think when they see a figure like this?

So get away from the view of Jesus you had as a child, and get to this mature, heavenly, majestic view; this is a view of Jesus as divine as well as human: in glory, in majesty, in purity, as well as in compassion. This is a new kind of Jesus to many, but if you are going to know the whole picture you must read this.

John is there, fallen before this figure, but now he realises it is the same Jesus on whose breast he once lay, because the same voice says what the voice had said many times on the Sea of Galilee, *'Fear not'*; at the graves of the dead, *'Fear not'*. The same voice that John knew sixty years before says, *'Fear not'*. And the same voice that said, *'I am the good shepherd'* and, *'I am the way and the truth and the life'* also says, *'I am the First and the Last'* — the same voice, same Jesus — meaning: I am always there, I am as eternal as God the Father. Secondly, he says, *'I was dead, and behold I am alive for ever and ever!'* John had seen Jesus on a cross, but here he is, sixty years later, still alive. Then the lovely thought as you see these keys that Jesus is carrying, he says, *'I hold the keys of death and Hades.'* This is why I look forward to the future. When the day comes when I am called to leave this world, I know that Jesus has the key; he can unlock death and let me out. This majestic, awe-inspiring figure speaks. Look again at the passage as a whole: *'Do not be afraid. I am the First and the Last. I am the Living One; I was dead, and behold I am alive for ever and ever! And I hold the keys of death and Hades.*

'Write, therefore, what you have seen, what is now and what will take place later. The mystery of the seven stars that you saw in my right hand and of the seven golden lampstands is this: The seven stars are the angels of the seven churches, and

the seven lampstands are the seven churches.'

A lampstand cannot give any light itself, it is only there to hold the light. A church cannot give any light, it is only there to hold Christ up so that he may shine. And a lampstand that loses its light is removed from its place, it is of no use, so Jesus is going to give John messages for those seven lampstands.

HIS OPINION OF CHURCHES
Revelation 2–3

In Revelation chapters 2–3 we have a series of seven short letters to seven churches in what we now know as Turkey, but which was then called Asia. If you look at a map you can see the province of Asia in the western part of Turkey and it is possible to find the churches. It is interesting that when you put them on a map you realise that the order of the churches is the order in which they would be reached by someone taking a circular tour. And the dear old apostle John, who was now serving a sentence in a prison on the island of Patmos, was clearly travelling around the churches, as he was accustomed to do when he was able. He is not able to do it in body now but he is doing it in spirit. We are now going to study the letter to the first church, which would have been the nearest – sixty miles straight across the sea from Patmos, the great port of Ephesus.

There is a kind of pattern in these seven churches in the letters addressed to them. Numbers one and seven are churches that are in great danger — something is seriously wrong with them. Number two and number six are grand churches that are in very good condition and are not criticised and numbers three, four and five in the middle are middling churches — they are a mixed bag. It is quite useful to remember these letters in that kind of 'sandwich' picture.

Now these letters are rather like the other letters to churches in the rest of the New Testament, the letters to the Ephesians, Philippians, Colossians, Thessalonians and so on, except first, they are much shorter and second, they are all sent to each church so that the church at Ephesus was able to hear what the letters to Smyrna and Pergamum and Thyatira said. That indicates that these little letters have more meaning than would be understood by the original church. In other words, these letters are for others and that is why they are here in the New Testament. They are for us to learn something from as well.

I want to mention an unusual kind of interpretation of these letters which does not convince me but has convinced a lot of people, and I must be fair and give it to you. This interpretation is that these seven letters represent seven periods in time in the history of the Christian church. For example, the church at Ephesus is seen as a picture of the first century, the church at Smyrna covers the persecution period of the second and third centuries; the church at Pergamum is the church of Constantine the emperor, Thyatira the Middle Ages, Sardis the Reformation, Philadelphia the church of the modern missionary movement beginning in the eighteenth century, and Laodicea a picture of the church of the twentieth/twenty-first centuries. Now that sounds very neat until you begin to look at it in detail.

Undoubtedly there are some striking parallels between each church and the century it is supposed to represent, but there are two difficulties. The first is that in any period in any century there are different churches of different character, and while the majority may be like one of these seven churches, some may be like the others; so while many churches today in England are like Laodicea there are many churches, thank God, that are not like Laodicea. So, you cannot just neatly categorise churches in time in this way. Furthermore, those who do this think only of the church in Europe and usually put Laodicea in the current century. I am not convinced by this interpretation which says the seven letters correspond to seven consecutive periods in history, and we are living in the last. I would rather say that

I believe these seven churches correspond to seven different kinds of church in space rather than in time, and that today in the twenty-first century, looking around what is happening to the church in the world, I can see Laodicean churches here, I can see Sardisian churches there, I can see Ephesian churches in the other place. In other words, in these seven churches you have a picture of every kind of church imaginable, and the question that we have to ask ourselves is this: which of these seven is your church? And therefore what has Christ to say to it? For here we are not looking at what other people think about the church, these letters are not from John, though he wrote them, they represent what Jesus thinks about the churches which are his, not ours, and his opinion may be exactly the opposite of everybody else's.

One of these churches was thought by people to be nearly dead, but actually they were on the point of new life. Another church had a name for being a live church, but in fact were dead. The most important opinion about your church is not my opinion or your opinion, or your town's opinion, or anyone else's opinion, the most important opinion is what Jesus thinks about us, and his opinion might be just the opposite of our own. As we read these seven letters, let us ask: Lord, is it I? I beg you not to think of any other church in your area — you have no business to and neither have I, and we are not to line up these seven churches with the numerous churches of our respective towns. What we are to do is to say: Lord, is that my church? If so, what have you got to say to me? Funnily enough, I have never yet come across a church that does not fit into one of these seven categories, as if the number seven, which is the complete number in scripture says: here is the total picture of the mixed bag that you will find if you go from church to church. With that introduction, please read the letter to the Ephesian church.

Ephesus (2:1ff.)

I think it would help you if I began by telling you a little about Ephesus as a town, just to paint the scene. You will have noticed that it is right on the coast, and it was in fact the main sea port of Asia; if you want a city in England that corresponds to it, you might think of Liverpool. All the trade from the east came right across the land bridge from the larger Asia, from India and China. The goods came to Ephesus and were shipped west from there. It was a very important city even if it was not the capital. However, the river was silting up, and in fact if you went to Ephesus today you would have to travel many miles inland because the silt brought down by the river Caster has filled in the old harbour and now there is land where once there was water.

It was a vast metropolis, a self-governing democracy all on its own. It was also a centre of religion. One of the seven wonders of the world was at Ephesus, the great temple of Artemis, towering above the whole city. And in and around that temple they sold some horrible little idols, a representation of a female goddess covered with breasts. This was Diana of the Ephesians, and there were many who had made a lot of money selling these idols to tourists. You may remember that Paul put them out of business when he started preaching in Ephesus. There was a museum here. It was a great sports centre; there were games held — the pan-Ionian games were held there every May and crowds came to the large stadium.

Pageants, a panorama of cultural life —this was the city.

Socially, it was extremely wealthy. The temple was a kind of safe deposit for valuables and people kept their jewels and money in the safe-keeping of the temple where the eunuchs and priestesses looked after it. As far as morality went, it was a city to which criminals naturally gravitated, indeed, they could have asylum in the temple of Artemis, so if you went to the temple you would be likely to meet most of the Asian criminals sooner or later, running away from some crime. The best summary I have heard of Ephesus is this: it was the vanity fair of Asia. Right there in the middle of vanity fair was a church, a church that had been blessed with about the best succession of ministers you could imagine. They had had St Paul as their minister for a start, and he had stayed longer there than anywhere else — two and a half years. You may remember the scene on the beach where the elders of the church broke down and wept, as did he when he had to leave them for the last time. So they had had Paul; they had had Priscilla and Aquila, that godly couple with great gifts; they had had Apollos, the man who was skilled in expounding the Old Testament; they had had the apostle John who was writing to them now. One historical record states that John was released from Patmos, from the island where he was in prison, and that in fact he came back to Ephesus as an old, broken man, and one Sunday morning they carried him into church on a stretcher and he was brought to the front of the church in Ephesus, this old man about to die, and he preached a sermon of three words to them. He said, '*Love one another*', and that is the story of the last minister they had — at least in the first century. So they had Paul, Apollos, Aquila and Priscilla and John, and if you had had a succession of ministers like that you would count yourself blessed! So right in the middle of vanity fair was this church that John is writing to, not with his own opinion, which might have been very different, but with Jesus' opinion of the church.

The letter begins like this: it is not addressed to the church but to the angel. There are two levels at which you may write letters: you can write at the human level — John to the church — or you can write a supernatural letter — Jesus to the angel. We must never forget that when we meet for worship the angels are meeting with us. It may well be — and I am speculating here on the basis of this text — that there is a guardian angel appointed by God to look after every church and to report to him. Some churches started guessing who their angel was and they called themselves the church of St Michael, or the church of St Gabriel, and some to go one better call themselves the church of All Angels, just to say we have got the lot of them looking after us! So they have vied with one another and people have said, 'Oh well, we'll go better than that, we'll call ourselves St Mary', or, 'We'll go one higher and say St Saviour'. I do not know the name of an angel looking after the church at which I was the pastor, I just know that the angels are real, that they are in touch with us even if we are not in touch with them.

This letter brings in the angel at the very beginning, as much as to say: you people at Ephesus, remember the angels are involved with you; they are watching your worship. Think of Paul's somewhat debated and controversial words about ladies wearing hats in church. The reason he gives for this is that the angels are watching, which is an intriguing reason that I will leave you to think about. But before I rush any further onto the ice that is rapidly getting thinner, I'll move on! The angels are watching over the churches. The letter hints at the very beginning: you can look at the church at the human level, but that is not enough. Look at it from the heavenly angle. What do the angels see? What does Jesus see? So Jesus writes to the angel. Even though the human beings are going to read the letter, it is clearly the angel who will watch whether they put right what is wrong; it is the angel who will remove the lampstand if the matter is not put right. And, in fact, though men can decide to open and close churches, angels can shut a church. We could build a new church, but an angel could close it, and if we were not doing our job then I pray that he would close it because there is nothing worse than a church remaining open after the Lord has departed from it.

The letter is addressed to the angel, but who from? *him who holds the seven stars in his right hand. . . .* There are some interesting words in the Greek language for *hold*; it means completely surround, so that you cannot get at it at all. He who holds the stars is the one who holds the churches like that. We are reminded of John 10:28 when Jesus speaks of his sheep — *'no-one can snatch them out of my hand.'* Jesus holds every church of his. It is a vivid word. There is only one person who can damage the church and that is Jesus, through his angels; he sometimes does, but nobody else can, not even the gates of Hades.

Not only does he hold the churches in his hands, which tells us of his protection, but he walks among them. This is intended to convey to us the idea that Jesus is the 'foreman'. If you go around a factory you will see some people not apparently working but walking around. If they are doing it for the valid, proper reason it is because they have been appointed to oversee what is going on, to see that a particular lathe or assembly line is working and being operated properly. Jesus walks among the churches and he looks to see if this church is doing its job, and that one is right and the other is fulfilling his purpose. It is a sobering thought that Jesus is walking among the churches, looking at them; it helps us to worship properly and seriously when we realise that he is the one who is watching, so he says in the letter, *I know*. He knows every single thing done and said in a church. That is an encouraging or a frightening thought, depending on what you are doing. Pascal, the great philosopher, once said this: 'If everybody knew what each said of the other, there wouldn't be four friends left in the world.' Let me apply that. Jesus knows everything each of us says about anyone else in the church; he says, *I know*. That is an awful thought if we gossip, but it is an encouragement too. Supposing your task in the church is a quiet one that nobody notices, there is no obvious reward, it is something done behind the scenes, and sometimes you wonder if it is ever appreciated or if it is worthwhile — he says, *I know*. He knows everything we all do: *I know*.

In this letter he commends them for three good things and refers to one bad thing. I think it is lovely the way Jesus always commends before he criticises. There is a cardinal rule for church meetings as for any other meeting: if you are going to criticise, say something good first; if you are going to condemn, commend something good first. He never condemns without commending first; and in the churches he criticises most of these seven, he also praises most. And as Jesus looked down on this church, what were the things he saw that thrilled him? A little beehive of a church at Ephesus; they were busy, they worked hard, they toiled, they did not grow weary; it was costly in time and energy, yet they gave exhausting service to the church and to the Lord. They were a busy, labouring church and they did not get tired of the jobs they were given. Thank God for churches that have people in them who do not tire of Christian service after a few weeks or months, but who are able to go on, and who toil and who labour without seeking for rest.

Secondly, there was their perseverance. They were under social pressure. They were being snubbed, ostracised, hated and even subject to physical violence, yet they were hanging on. Some of the shopkeepers in the church had lost their customers since they became Christians, others were not even allowed to buy in certain shops in the town. How would you feel if somebody said, 'Oh, you go to that church down the road; sorry, I'm not doing any business with you'? That is what was happening here, but they were enduring it and that thrilled Jesus. The third thing: they were an enlightened church; they hated error and evil. It may seem strange to you that Jesus commends a church for hating, but a healthy church hates certain things. First of all, it hates evil in its members and it deals with that. Second, it hates false doctrine in its preachers, and it deals with that too. And third, it hates new movements and sects which teach people wrong behaviour. The Nicolaitans were such and they were teaching that Christianity and licentiousness went together, and this church hated that. Now, let us ask what things our churches hate, and whether we hate the right things.

There was a movement in the twentieth century which actually linked Jesus and 'free love' and said the two go together. That was identical with the Nicolaitan heresy which the Ephesians hated; they felt it such a slander and a blasphemy against the name of Christ that they loathed it. If you really are a healthy church you hate sin in members, you hate false doctrine in preachers and you hate movements that sweep young people away into perverted behaviour, into thinking that it does not matter how you behave as long as you believe in Jesus. These are things that they hated, so Jesus commends them. But looking down on this church, his x-ray eyes saw a flaw.

I remember going into a car factory and an inspector of a machine part looked at it, rejected it and threw it out, though to my amateur eye it looked perfectly alright. He then said, 'Ah, but look at this', and he showed me a little flaw that would have endangered the lives of those who drove that car. Just a little flaw he had spotted, and out it went. Jesus looked at this church and drew attention to a flaw. What he found is something that could close your church, even though there may be many good things about it, and it is so simple: this church had lost its first love — that is all — and this is the most tragic thing that can happen to a church.

This church had been there for forty years, and that is long enough for the second generation of Christians to come along, and second generation Christians can so easily fall below the first generation. That is the one big danger of being brought up in a Christian home; it is the one big danger of a church where there are families and the church is kept going with the next generation — that the first love goes. From one point of view you can love the Lord more if you were a criminal or a cannibal or some terrible person before you came to Christ than if you were brought up within church. The first love can be so much deeper if you realise just how much Christ has saved you from. This was a second generation church and the first love had gone.

What love had gone? Was it the love for their neighbour?

It may well have been. They had stopped loving the people outside as they had once done. They were comfortable within the church, they had a grand time and they were beginning to forget the hundreds of thousands of people outside the doors of the church, they had stopped loving them and trying to win them for Christ — it could have been that. More important, it could be their love for each other, and Moffat translates this passage, *you have given up loving each other as you did at the first*. Their intimacy and interest in each other was flagging. But I think the deepest root love which they had lost was their love for their Lord. You see, if you really love the Lord you will love one another and love your neighbour — the three are bound up as one, you cannot separate them. If you do not love your brother whom you have seen, how can you say you love the Lord whom you have not seen? These three loves are all one.

I remember going into a house many miles from where I lived, and in that house there was a proud housewife (or a houseproud wife, should I put it that way?) It was spotless, a museum of domestic science. I nearly wrote 'domestic silence' because that would have fitted too. When the husband came home from work he went into that home as if it were a Hindu temple; all his shoes were laid up in the porch. When I called, a dust sheet had to come off the chair before I sat on it. No dust ever got into that home, I should think it was too frightened! It was subject to imminent execution. There was always a duster handy. It was a beautiful home and you could have taken a picture of any room for a magazine. It had not always been like that. The husband did not like coming home one bit, so he usually came home late. There had been a time, in the first rapture after their marriage, when the furniture had taken second place. The furniture was for them both to sit on and love each other, but that had gone — the first careless rapture had gone. Now it was a beautiful house but it was no longer a home. It was not a place where people could relax.

This church, too, was perfectly kept. There was no dirt there, it was well-run, people were busy doing things, it was active and efficient, there was just an absence of love. That is tragic when it happens in a home — and it happens more often than we care to think — but when it happens in a church it is terrible. It is not a loving home, it has become sterile. There is a time to relax and love, and Jesus is telling this church that this was the missing thing that he was looking for, and if it did not come back then they would be closed down, despite all their people, their labours, their busyness, their activity, their purity of doctrine and purity of life — even with all of that, it was not a place that people would want to come to; it was a church from which the lampstand would be removed. They had forgotten their first careless love; they had left the honeymoon behind. That should never happen with the Lord; we should always be on honeymoon with Jesus. We should always have that rapture and that love which we had at first.

That was what was wrong and it was the only thing he saw that was wrong, yet it was enough to bring that church to extinction. He tells them how to put it right, in three steps.

First, they are to *remember*. How many husbands have said to wives, and wives have said to husbands, 'Do you remember what we were like ten, twenty years ago?' And Jesus says to them: *'Remember the height from which you have fallen!'* They need to recall how it was when they first loved him. If you are an older Christian — I am not trying to lay it on too thick, and I say this humbly — was there a time in your life when you could not be kept away from a prayer meeting? When, if somebody said, 'Let's go out and evangelise', you were the first volunteer? Was there a time when you were so much in love with Jesus that you wanted to tell the world? What has happened to the first love? Was there a time when you loved to be with other Christians, and if there was a fellowship meeting you were there, but now you would rather stay at home and watch television (you are tired after a long day)? Remember, remember.

Second, *repent*. That does not just mean say sorry, it means turn right around, make a clean break with where you are now.

Third: *do the things you did at first*. May I suggest that husbands and wives who have got a little away from each other go back and spend a weekend, maybe where you had your honeymoon or a special holiday together. Get somebody to look after the children, do what you need to do, but go back, start again. And a church that has lost its love, remember what you used to be like, get back there, repent and repeat the things you did at first. If you used to love to go to those things, then go back to them, rekindle the love. Where is the blessedness I knew when first I saw the Lord? Loss of first love is what had happened to Ephesus, and a church in which this has happened is finished in Jesus' sight, even if it is busy and active. Well, that is the remedy and it is clear enough.

Finally, there are two things to note about this letter. First, we are told that if they did not get back to that first love, Jesus would remove their lampstand. What happened to the church at Ephesus? We do not know from the Bible, but from other sources there is evidence that they went back to their first love. In the second century AD a saintly man called Ignatius wrote in a letter, 'I am just thrilled with your love for the Lord and for each other' — so they got back, but they did not stay there. The church at Ephesus, in the third century AD, lost its love again. A twentieth century tourist went to Ephesus — it is only a village now, and in the whole village only a few people called themselves Christians, and they hardly knew anything about Paul or John. That is all that was left, and it was once one of the most thriving churches. I do not know how long it will be before Christ comes back, but I hope and pray that when he comes there will still be a church in my town, loving in the first careless rapture until he comes back — full of love for the Lord, love for each other and love for neighbour.

The other thing that Jesus says is this: *To him who overcomes, I will give the right to eat from the tree of life, which is in the paradise of God.* If they did get back to their first love, they could look forward to eating from the tree of life in paradise — and the word *paradise* means the King's garden, the special place in the kingdom. They would have such an experience of heaven, which is full of love. The words *love* and *heaven* go together even in pop songs at the human level. But at the divine level, when a church loves, that church is a little bit of heaven, it is beginning to taste paradise, and it looks forward even more to eating of the tree of life.

The last word is this: *He who has an ear, let him hear what the Spirit says to the churches.* So what is written would be a sheer waste of time unless we listen, unless we get on our knees and say to God, 'Where is the blessedness I knew when first I saw the Lord? Am I settling down to middle-aged respectability? Is our church settling down because I am? Lord, what do you see in our church, a busy active church seeking purity of life and doctrine but lacking love? If that is what you see Lord, help me to remember what it used to be like, help me to repent of what I have become and help me to repeat what I did at first. *Amen.*'

Smyrna (2:8ff.)

While we study these letters, we may ask which of the churches is like our own. If we live in Britain, we must begin by saying it is not Smyrna. Here, we are not about to be thrown in prison. It is the easiest thing in the world for us to go to church, and the easiest thing to stay in bed, and we take for granted that we can worship unhindered. Smyrna was not like that. Let me give you some background on the town. We are now moving north. John is in prison but his thoughts were moving around the seven churches — from Ephesus to Smyrna and then to Pergamum, which is the next town on a circular trip round the churches of Asia Minor. Today Smyrna is named Izmir and it is the third largest city in Turkey in terms of population (once its nine urban districts have been taken into account). Of this there is still a small Christian population in a country that is over 99% Muslim. This is in contrast to the town of Ephesus which is only a village and only has a few Christians in it. You will remember that Jesus said that if his hearers did not keep their love he would remove the lampstand, but a suffering church tends to have a much longer life than a church that loses its love. The Christianity of the town is largely of the Eastern Orthodox variety, and this varies of course in quality tremendously, but there is no doubt about it that there are still many of Christ's people in Smyrna — even today, after two thousand years.

It is one of the most beautiful towns in Turkey — it still is beautiful and it was even more so then. The reason is that some few hundred years before Jesus was born the whole town was destroyed — rather like Coventry during World War II — and they were able to re-plan a new town, and the greatest town planners of the day created a plan that laid out boulevards and squares. A large, conical hill gives a wonderful backcloth, and it really is a beautiful city, founded as it was a thousand years before Christ. It is now three thousand years old, continuously inhabited.

It was a cultured city with a stadium and a library, and one of the greatest thinkers of the world was born there, a man called Homer. His monument stands to this day in the middle of the town. It was wealthy, it had a harbour, trade came through this town. The most important thing we should highlight is that it was an intensely patriotic town. In the past, if you had taken a British coin out of your pocket you would have seen Britannia on some of the coins — a copy of a Roman goddess; and you can see an almost exact replica of Britannia in the temples erected to the goddess of Rome, and the first one ever built was built at Smyrna. They became so loyal to the Roman emperor that it was here they began to think he was god, and they were worshipping the emperor long before Christ was born. That was going to prove difficult for the Christians. Here was a city that was full of earthly pride and honour, and there was no doubt that when a little church began to be in that city they would be despised, criticised and ultimately persecuted, and that is what happened.

We look first at their suffering. What caused it? Why did they have to suffer? The answer is that they suffered because they lived in a town full of Romans and full of Jews, and neither Roman nor Jew liked the Christian. Why did the Roman not like the Christian? For a start, Christians were not very patriotic. They prayed for the emperor, they were good citizens in that they did not knowingly break the law, they were not criminals, but one thing they would not do was to bow down and worship Caesar. They said there is only one person that we will bow down before, and that is the Lord Jesus. The Romans did not like that, it seemed like a lack of patriotism in a very loyal city, and the Christians did not fit in to the pattern. But the worst suffering came from the Jews. I know there has been a lot of anti-Semitism in Christian history and it is a painful thing, but there is another side to that and it is this: Jewish anti-Christianism. It has been as terrible as anti-Semitism. During the early centuries no-one hated the Christians more than the Jews, no-one caused them more trouble. You study the life of Paul, and again and again he was in prison, he was beaten, he was stoned, not because of the Romans but because the Jews set the Romans onto him, and there were plenty of Jews in Smyrna. There was a whole colony, many were engaged in business, and many hated those Christians. This was a peculiar situation. The Romans said, you must worship Caesar — and everybody did, except for the Jews. Of all the people in Smyrna there was one select group that had special permission not to worship Caesar and they were the Jews. They were very jealous of that, and they did not want to lose that privilege. Now, here was another group, tagging on, jumping on their bandwagon, refusing to worship Caesar. What did they do? They reported the Christians to the Romans and they made life intolerable for the Christians.

Let us ask why, generally, people do not suffer for being Christian in the United Kingdom. There are two possible reasons, and I ask you to judge which is true or the main one. The first would be that the church has influenced the nation in this country and that in fact Christian standards have so influenced our society that they do not see us as all that different from themselves, and therefore because people outside would call themselves 'Christian' they do not persecute us. That is one reason, that the church has influenced the world a great deal. The other possible reason, which I ask you to consider carefully, is that the world has influenced the church too much.

Either way, it means that there is not enough difference between church and world for there to be a head-on clash. Which do you think it is? It could be a bit of both. I am only going to say, because I believe it is largely true (of my own life as well as yours), that it is our fault, and that the world has influenced us too much. Young people are saying today, 'We look at people who go to church and we don't see any difference between them and their godless neighbours. They have the same ambitions, the same desires, the same covetousness.' One thing is absolutely clear: the more different you are from the community in which you live, the more you will be persecuted. I have the feeling that the reason it is so relatively comfortable for us — while it is partly due to living in a so-called 'Christian country' — is largely due to the fact that we go along with the community too far. We are not different enough. Where you live at closer quarters with people outside the church, persecution occurs. If you join the army and you go into a barrack room and you do not swear and you do not tell dirty jokes, you will be persecuted very quickly because you are different, and society does not like those misfits who do not go along with others.

If we look at what Christians were suffering in Smyrna, it is pretty frightening. They had already suffered financial poverty. They had lost their money. How many of us would still be Christians if we lost all our money — if we knew that we would be beggars for going to a service? Let us be honest with ourselves, the word that is used here for poverty means to be utterly destitute of everything — not just to have the old age pension and no more, but to have nothing, and therefore to be reduced to begging from people who hate you. The church in Smyrna had been reduced to poverty; they had nothing to put in the collection on Sunday, and it was because they were Christians.

Secondly, they had suffered slander — verbal persecution. I do not know if you can take that. There used to be a proverb that said, 'sticks and stones may break your bones, but names will never hurt you.' I do not think that is true. I think you can put up with sticks and stones but it is awfully difficult when people talk about you and say all manner of evil against you falsely — to bear it for Christ's sake. You are tempted all the time to justify yourself and say 'we are not like that.' But this is what they were suffering. They were accused of cannibalism because they talked of eating the body and drinking the blood of Jesus Christ at the breaking of bread. They were accused of having sexual orgies because they held meetings which they called 'love feasts'. When they walked down the street, they could see people nudging each other and pointing, and they knew what kind of thing they were saying. That is tough.

Jesus told them about something worse that would happen. Some of those slandered, poverty-stricken people in Smyrna were going to prison. Prison *can* be a very holy and heavenly place. When General Booth's daughter was imprisoned she wrote a hymn, and this is one verse: *Best beloved of my soul, I am here alone with thee, and my prison is a heaven, since thou sharest it with me*. Then Jesus goes further in this letter, telling them that they were to be faithful *even to the point of death*. Some would be executed for their faith in him.

I have only once been a minister of a church in which there were members who died for Christ, literally. It had a profound effect on everybody else, believe me. When we baptised an Arab we knew that we were signing his death warrant, and we knew that there would be those who would so hate him that they would kill him. I remember one RAF boy coming to me after finding this out and saying, 'I have never met anybody before who was prepared to die for his faith; I just can't believe it.' He said, 'I have been to church for many years, but I have never met anybody like that.'

We may put 'unto death' on gravestones, meaning that somebody was a faithful Christian right until the day they died, but *Be faithful, even to the point of death* means more than being faithful all your life, it means dying for the Lord, and they were going to know martyrdom.

One of the martyrs of the church of Smyrna was a man called Polycarp, who when he was in extreme old age was burned at the stake. The Jews hated him so much they broke the Sabbath to gather the wood for the bonfire on which he was burned. Polycarp was tied to the stake because he refused to deny Christ, even though he was a grey-haired old man, and not a man who could take much suffering. The proconsul of Smyrna said to him, 'Deny Christ and you can go free. I beg you as an old man consider your grey hairs.' And Polycarp replied like this: 'Eighty and six years have I served Christ and he never did me any injury, how then can I blaspheme my King and Saviour?' And then later he said to the proconsul, 'Thou threatenest me with fire which burns for an hour and after a little while is extinguished, but art ignorant of the fire of the coming judgement and the eternal punishment reserved for the ungodly.'

So at eighty-six he died. A wind came and blew the flames away from him, so a merciful soldier ran in and strangled him. But that was Polycarp of this very church, an old man, but he was not going to deny Christ, even for the sake of a few peaceful years in his old age. This is the stuff of which the church is made. The blood of the martyrs is the seed of the church, and where the church is like this it grows. In a sense we should not pity the church in China, or indeed the church in Turkey today, but the church within our own borders — it is ourselves we should pity, that we lack the stimulus that comes from being in this situation.

What did Jesus have to say to this church that was enduring terrible suffering and was going to go through worse? He says a number of things to comfort them and enable them to surmount their problems. First he says, *'I know your afflictions'*. One of the hardest things when you are suffering is that you feel that nobody knows what you are going through. I was once told by a man who was helping Czechoslovak Christians, when that country was under communist control, 'I see the answers to the prayers of people in England for Czechoslovakia — they do not'; and only in eternity will be revealed all the answers to our prayers for those people. We do not know what is happening, we do not know how our prayers are being answered, but God is answering our prayers for the oppressed peoples in the world today. Now Jesus says, *I know* — nobody else might know but he knows. In a sense he means something more than I know about your tribulations, he knew what they were going through because he had been through it. Nobody can know what another suffers unless they have suffered the same way. You can sympathise but you cannot suffer with somebody unless you have been through the same thing. The black slaves of the southern states of America went through terrible troubles and they used to sing, 'Nobody knows the trouble I've seen, nobody knows but Jesus.' The people in China know that we are praying for them, but they know that we do not know, and they sing like this too. Nobody knows but Jesus.

Jesus reminds the church that he *'died and came to life again'*. Of every other human being you have to say he lived and he died — of Jesus only can you say he died and he lives. So here is a comfort for them: he is teaching them this — they were looking forward to living and dying, but he was the one who died and lives; he knew, and he was going to help them into the future.

Then he warns them that some people who said that they were Jews were not, but that they belonged to the devil. A certain synagogue was satanic. That was a strong statement. There has long been a debate about the definition of a Jew. Are you aware of this debate? Can a man who does not believe in the Jewish faith be a Jew? That was the question. It was a comfort to these Christians that Jesus saw the devil in the synagogue that was reporting them to the Romans.

The next thing he teaches is that their suffering would have a limit on it — ten days, he says, which is a round period rather than an exact term. And it would test them, which does not mean that it would break them, but that it would bring them through triumphant and strong. Then he teaches them that they may be poor but they are really rich. If you lost all your money, how much would you be worth? These people were as millionaires in God's sight. The treasure laid up for them in heaven is enormous. The real wealth of a man is not to be measured in his bank balance — it is the world that thinks that way — the real wealth of a man is his riches in Christ. Jesus teaches them not to worry about their poverty: they were rich; they were going to inherit all that Jesus gives.

Some people think it is a horrible thing to die — well, it is, without Christ; but there is something more horrible than dying, there is something to be afraid of far more than death. What? The second death. Jesus said what that was. He said, *'Do not be afraid of those who kill the body but cannot kill the soul. Rather, be afraid of the One who can destroy both soul and body in hell'* (Matthew 10:28). That is the second death. It is one thing to be killed physically, but to be killed spiritually is terrible.

Jesus says, *'Be faithful, even to the point of death, and I will give you the crown of life.'* Smyrna had a large stadium, and when a man won a race and came victorious to the tape he was crowned. Honour and dignity and joy were his and the crowd cheered — he had won through. Jesus was teaching that if you are faithful to death and lay down your life he will be waiting with the crown, and the whole world will know that you won through. So he says, *'Do not be afraid of what you are about to suffer.'* Jesus was always telling people not to be afraid because he knew that fear cripples. Fear leads people to do silly things, fear leads people to deny Christ, but he is telling them not to be afraid, the future is in his hands, not Satan's; Jesus will have the last word. *He who has an ear, let him hear what the Spirit says to the churches.* I believe that the day is coming in Britain, and maybe within my lifetime, when we shall suffer in Britain. I am sure it is coming because Britain is moving further and further away from Christ and unless we compromise our church life and our Christian standards, and if we remain faithful, it may well be that some of us in our respective churches will be called to be faithful unto death. Maybe then we will turn back to the letter to Smyrna and thank Jesus for writing it.

Pergamum (2:12ff.)

Back in the days of the Cold War it was my privilege to visit East Berlin. There were a number of things that I wanted to see in that half of the city, but the most interesting thing was in a museum. It was in a room about the size of the civic hall in Guildford and there was only one thing in the room — it had to be that size because it was so big — it was Satan's throne from Pergamum. Inside this gigantic room there has been carried, stone by stone from Pergamum, Satan's throne, referred to here in Revelation 2. After the Russians took Berlin they carried it all the way to Moscow, later they carried it back again and rebuilt it. Imagine a staircase, probably twice as wide as a typical church building. There is a gigantic stairway which rises right in the middle, and then at the top is a marvellous temple with Corinthian pillars all around it, and a frieze of sculptured figures of gods and goddesses. That stood above Pergamum on the top of a hill and it was the centre of pagan worship for this town. You can still go and see that thing in Berlin and it makes you shudder. The very size of it! I walked up those steps and thought: Paul walked through here once, maybe he walked up these very stones. But certainly John preached not far from these stones and he saw this overpowering temple devoted to pagan gods.

That was not the only pagan thing in Pergamum. It was the centre of the worship of the Greek god Asclepius. If you have ever seen the badge of the Royal Army Medical Corps you will notice that it is a pole with a serpent entwined around it, and the serpent is Asclepius, the old pagan god of healing, and the serpent was worshipped in Pergamum — it was the Lourdes of the ancient world; people came here to be healed and healings took place. Satan can heal, and healings take place through spiritualist seances, and Satan has the power over your body, both to bring you disease and to bring you health. The trouble is that if ever he brings you health he damns your soul in so doing and wrecks your spiritual life. This was the kind of pagan atmosphere in Pergamum. Mind you, it was very literate, very cultured, they had a library of 200,000 books at Pergamum and it was in Pergamum that parchment was invented ('parchment' is a shortened form of *pergamene charta*), on which you could write instead of the clay tablets and stone monuments that they had used before. It was a marvellous place, but towering over it was Satan's throne, this hilltop covered with temples of all kinds where people came for physical health. In this little city there was a church, and it had a tough time.

Looking through the letter that Jesus sends to the church, he commends two things. First of all he says, *'you remain true to my name'*. They would not let go the name by which they had found health. They did not deny the faith, and it looks as if there came a crisis to that church because the verb means they did not deny the faith *once*, and it looks as if a great crisis came when they were tempted to deny the faith and they did not do it. One man in the church paid for it with his life. His name was Antipas — a very interesting name because it means *anti* (against), *pas* (all). It is an appropriate name because being a Christian he was against all, and they were all against him — there was a complete breakdown and he was killed for the faith.

So they already had their first martyr. This was the first of the seven churches to have a martyr. Smyrna was warned that they would have, but they had none as yet. But here in Pergamum the first man to die for the faith had already given his blood. You would have thought that Jesus would have just comforted them, but he did not. He comforted Smyrna and he did not say a thing against them, but when he came to Pergamum he said, *'I have a few things against you'*. The church had held on to his name in that town of pagan worship. But they were already compromising their belief and behaviour. They were letting pagan beliefs and pagan behaviour influence them more than they realised. This is how Satan can get hold of a church. It may not be through direct, frontal attack, but through worming his way in through your behaviour and your doctrine.

Let me just tell you why he refers to Balaam. I am sure you have heard of Balaam's ass that spoke. Balaam himself was an 'ass' in what he did not say. If you know the story of Balaam you will know that he was called upon by Balak, king of Moab, who was against Israel, to prophesy a curse of God upon Israel to help him to win a battle, offering him a lot of money to do so. Balaam tried, but he could not get the words out. Balak tried again through emissaries, and Balaam said, *'Even if Balak gave me his palace filled with silver and gold, I could not do anything great or small to go beyond the command of the LORD my God.'* But Israel suffered a defeat in another way. The Moabite women began to attract the men of Israel, the people of God married pagans, and they began to get interested in the religion of the women; they lowered their behaviour sexually, and Israel lost the war with Moab. The lesson to be learned from all this is that a frontal attack of Satan can usually be beaten off because you recognise it, but

Satan comes around another way, and he will if possible get you into a personal relationship in which you must lower your standards of belief and behaviour. That is what happened here in Pergamum. They had faced dying for the faith and they still talked about Jesus — but they were beginning to eat idol meat, and they were fornicating.

In other words, their standards of belief and behaviour were going down steadily. They were going down because of a group of people called the Nicolaitans, whose teaching could be summed up quite simply like this: we must not be narrow-minded, we must not be puritanical, we must not catch the disease of religious mania or scruples; we must not lose our relationships with the world or our reputation because we want to win them; we can have mental reservations but the thing is to go as far as we can in a worldly direction to win the world for Christ. That was their teaching, and the result was that Christians, while they still talked about Jesus, became mixed up with idol worship, and with lower moral standards, and the church at Pergamum was going down.

I think this is relevant to us if the letter to Smyrna is not. We are living in a pagan Britain. Just go and look at any bookstall or study the posters on any tube train, and you do not need any further persuading. It is Pergamum all over again. I recall taking part in one television programme in Manchester and found that although they had invited me there to talk about the Christian faith, they had invited witches, astrologers, spiritists, humanists, agnostics, atheists, who had not got the first clue about the Christian faith, and this is the kind of pagan mixture that we find ourselves in now in this country of ours.

Not only is idolatry coming back in the form of magic, occultism, spiritism and magazines that dabble in all kinds of things, but the standards of behaviour are clearly going down. If Satan does not get us by martyring us he could get us this way, by Christians anxious to keep as near to the world as possible and therefore gradually lowering their standards; by the people of God marrying those who do not belong to God — and hard though it is to say it, it were better to remain unmarried than to get unequally yoked to a person who does not belong to Jesus.

This is how the church in Britain could get into Satan's hands in the immediate future — not by Satan killing us all, not by the Prime Minister sending us all to the Colosseum or its equivalent, but by an infiltration of mixed beliefs and mixed behaviour leading us into the kind of relationship where we must lower our standards. Already, I think, most of us who are Christians today do things that would horrify our grandfathers, and we must face the fact that although we think they were old-fashioned, and although we dismiss them as narrow-minded, many of them had a clearer grasp of Christian belief and behaviour than we have.

Jesus had a very strong message: he commanded repentance. *'Repent therefore! Otherwise, I will soon come to you and will fight against them with the sword of my mouth.'* It is bad enough having Romans against you and Jews against you, and pagans against you, but the most terrible persecution a church can have is when Jesus is against you. Why is he so fierce with them? There were those amongst them who were sinning and holding to false teaching. *'You have people there who . . . .'* and, *'Likewise, you also have those who . . . .'* A church like that is not only not a help to Jesus, it is a positive hindrance; a church like that is an embarrassment to him, a church like that, far from being an advertisement for Christianity, becomes

71

precisely the opposite, and even pagan people can see, and they say, 'Well, if that is Christianity I do not want anything to do with it.'

As I study these letters I discover in each of them a mark of a true church. In the letter to Ephesus it must be a loving church; in the letter to Smyrna it will be a suffering church; in the letter to Pergamum a true church must be a separated, disciplined church. There will be things that we cannot do as Christians that our neighbours and friends are going to be doing quite freely. There will be standards that we cannot stoop to because we are Christians, if we are going to survive as a lampstand shining in a dark place. I see this letter as more than relevant, to *him who overcomes* [those who keep straight in a crooked world, who keep clean in a dirty world, who keep Christian in a pagan world], Jesus says that he will give two things. The first is *hidden manna*. What does he mean?

I am guessing here, and I can only go as far as my own opinion, and tell you that I think he is saying something like this. The 'manna' originally was food from heaven from God that kept them going through the wilderness, and what he is saying means this: if you live as you ought, you are going to miss a whole lot of things that the world offers; you are going to feel that the world is a wilderness to you, that there is not much you can have, then I will see that you get satisfaction from God. He will give you a hidden manna that nobody else will see. Every day he will give you nourishment, something to refresh you, something to satisfy you. While the world around you is satisfying itself in so many pagan ways, he will give you hidden manna.

The second thing he says he will give to *'him who overcomes'* is *'a white stone'*. There are a number of possibilities as to what this means. Sometimes when a person was acquitted by a jury they would vote by putting a black or a white stone into a jar, then they counted up the white stones — it could mean acquittal. Sometimes a white stone was a symbol of a happy day — we talk about a red letter day, they talked about a white stone day. Sometimes a white stone was a ticket to get free food in the dole queue; sometimes it was a lucky charm; it may have been some other popular local superstition, I do not know. I think the important thing is what is written on it. Jesus says, *'I will also give him a white stone with a new name written on it, known only to him who receives it.'* At its very simplest that says to me that we can be told secrets. If we keep straight and clean in a pagan world, he can tell us things not shared generally. There can be talk at an intimate level about things hidden from other people, and in particular about a new name. The 'new name' could mean one of two things. It could mean that Jesus will give a new name as when he said, *'You are Simon son of John. You will be called Cephas' (which, when translated, is Peter);* and when he called James and his brother John *Sons of Thunder.* He may mean that if you keep clean he will give you a special name he will call you, just to make this intimate relationship precious, as when a couple get married they invariably develop some little name for each other that they keep to themselves, and they do not tell anybody else, it is just a secret relationship, a pet name for each other.

If we keep straight in a crooked world, he regards us as very close to him, we can have secret names for each other, we can have intimacy with him. You will lose your friends in the world, but you can be closer to him. You will lose your pagan superstition but you can have hidden manna from him. Even though you will lose out on many things by keeping true to Christ, the compensation is worth it; you receive far more than you lose.

So he says again, *'He who has an ear, let him hear what the Spirit says to the churches.'* Did you really get the message? Listen hard and do something about it, because it is the Spirit speaking to the churches.

Thyatira (2:18ff.)

We are making a circular tour of seven churches of Asia — what we now call western Turkey — and we come now to the fourth church, Thyatira. It is the smallest and least important of the seven towns, yet Jesus sends a longer letter to them than to anybody else. Is that not characteristic? Those whom others would dismiss as relatively unimportant, Jesus treats with greater care, so he sends a longer letter.

Let me tell you a little about this town. Virtually the only thing important about it was that you passed through it; it was at a junction of two valleys. This gave it its very slight significance. Two things were characteristic of this little town. First of all, it had a garrison, a barracks of soldiers to guard the junction. Secondly, it had a market. There was one speciality sold in this market that you could not freely get anywhere else: purple cloth. It was wool cloth dyed with an extract taken from shellfish, which produced the most marvellous purple material. It was almost certainly cloth from Thyatira which was used to mock our Lord when they put a purple robe on him. Royalty came to Thyatira for this purple cloth. There was a famous businesswoman who exported from Thyatira — her name was Lydia, a seller of purple from Thyatira, who went over to Macedonia where Paul met her, you may remember.

Here were the two things, and from a civilian point of view, of course, it was not the barracks but the market and the trade that really was the important thing. That gives you the background.

But there was one characteristic of social life in Thyatira which lies behind this letter — the trade guilds. If you take a trade union, a chamber of commerce and a Freemasons' lodge and mix them up together you have a trade guild — that is roughly what they were. And if you wanted to survive in Thyatira you had to belong to one, you had to join up, otherwise it was commercial suicide. But it involved you in all kinds of secret ceremonies, and therein arose the problem. Jesus writes to them and he particularly reminds them of his eyes and his feet — eyes which can blaze; eyes which search the mind and the heart; eyes which can see everything that goes on. I knew a man in the ministry who went into the ministry because a preacher once came to his home church where he and two other boys were playing cards in the back pew below the hymnbook shelf and they thought that nobody could see. Then, in the middle of the sermon, the preacher stopped and said, 'You three boys playing cards in the back pew, when are you going to come to Christ?' And he came to Christ at that service. He became a minister and his brother became a missionary. You would be amazed what the preacher can see! We have an advantage in that we may be six feet above criticism, but we see most that goes on. But the Lord sees everything that goes on. I can only see what the congregation is doing on the outside, but he can see what you are doing inside: how you feel, whether you are loving or hating it, whether you are listening or whether you are thinking of yesterday's football match or today's dinner.

Jesus searches the mind and the heart, and he was letting them know that he sees and knows what is really going on.

'I know your deeds, your love and faith, your service and perseverance . . . . ' And he could see members under pressure, outside and inside the church.

The pressure from outside was to join the trade guilds. They could not even open a shop unless they belonged to a trade guild in the town and the trouble was that it involved them in a number of activities, mainly dinners. Now what is wrong with dinners? Nothing, unless you eat too much! But before and after the dinners certain things happened in the trade guilds. Before the dinner they had a pagan ceremony and they offered meat to idols and said grace to a heathen god. After the dinner the fun began and it usually finished up in a pretty wild orgy. If you did not join in these trade guild dinners, pagan ceremonies beforehand and the immoral ceremonies afterwards, your business was finished and there was no other employment for you, unless you joined the garrison and became a soldier. That was life in Thyatira, and this pressure was forcing church members to get involved in things that they should never have been involved in.

I take a modern parallel, because I think it is a parallel and I only express my personal conviction that it is impossible to be a good Christian and find your faith compatible with the religious side of freemasonry, but many have become masons for social reasons and for other reasons without thinking of the religious side in which they will become involved and without asking: is that compatible with my Christian faith? This is the kind of pressure that was on the Thyatiran Christians. They could not do business unless they joined the guild; they did not do it seriously, they had to go through the ceremony, but then they did not believe in it. Was that not alright? Tertullian, who came and preached to them, said it was not alright. The members came to him afterwards and said, 'But we must live, we have got to live.' And he said, 'Must you live?' There are no musts to Christian faith. It may sound a bit harsh but he was fighting for a church that was to be strong and pure.

The other pressure they had on them was inside the church. They had all this pressure outside, but there was a fifth column inside the church in the shape of one woman who was encouraging the men of the church to join in committing certain sins. It would be intriguing to guess who is referred to. Some have felt it was the pastor's wife, others have thought it was the wife of a prominent member of the church. Whoever it was, there was a woman in the church urging men to get into various sins, and joining in herself. Furthermore, a most damning indictment, Jesus mentions this Jezebel's claim to be a prophetess. She was encouraging people to dabble in areas which Jesus termed *'Satan's so-called deep secrets'*. All kinds of terrible results came from this woman's activity. We need to beware of false prophets and false prophetesses — particularly the latter, who have been the greater danger in church history. One thinks of people like Mary Baker Eddy and Annie Besant and so many others, who have said, 'I have a new revelation from God' and the 'revelation' contradicts what God has formerly said —and God never contradicts himself. The God who said, 'idolatry is wrong' would never, through a prophetess, tell you it was alright; and the God who said that you must not commit adultery or fornication would never have given this Jezebel words that contradicted his commands. Jesus calls her a Jezebel because there was a lady in the Old Testament who married the king of Israel, became the wife of the leader of God's people, and corrupted, not only her husband, but a whole nation by bringing other practices, both idolatrous and immoral, into the palaces, and when the palace goes wrong the rest of the country will follow suit. How important it is to pray for the Royal Family and to pray for the example that they must set.

So this was a sad situation, a difficult one. Jesus' message meant that he had given this woman time to repent, but she had not done so, therefore she would have to face his feet — burnished bronze feet which trample underfoot the enemies of God. She had been given her opportunities, she would not take them, and she had to go; her bed of sin would become a bed of sickness, and her partners and her children would go down with her.

But then Jesus turns to those members of this church who *'do not hold to her teaching and have not learned Satan's so-called deep secrets'* with words that assure them that it is not hopeless — *'hold on to what you have until I come.'* The church needed to hold fast to what they knew to be true, cut themselves off from this woman, cut themselves off from those trade guilds; whatever it cost, they had to hold fast. He was not going to lay on them any other burden, he was not going to make his words stricter to them, nor to give them new regulations.

They would be given three things. First, authority. The promise is that if we control ourselves now we will control others later; if we rule passions now, Jesus will allow us to rule people later. In other words, the man who can control himself is the man who is fit to lead others, and in the new heaven and the new earth there will be positions of leadership and responsibility. There will be those who rule, and they will be those who have ruled themselves here with discipline.

Secondly, power.

'He will rule them with an iron sceptre;
he will dash them to pieces like pottery'

One of the little side industries of Thyatira was pottery, and in fact to this very day you can go to Thyatira and see a pottery, and the inspector in the pottery looking at a vase if he saw a flaw would take a rod of iron and he would smash the vase. Josiah Wedgwood would spend his days going around his pottery smashing most of the things that had been made so that his reputation might be lifted. Jesus says of *'him who overcomes and does my will to the end'* that, *'He will rule them with an iron sceptre'*. What does he mean? He means this: as the world, the trade guilds and Jezebel have been breaking the church, one day he will give them the power to break those things. It is a solemn fact that although at the moment the pressures of the world are breaking Christians, there will come a day when Christians will break those pressures with a rod of iron, such as breaks the pottery into pieces.

And finally, glory. *'I will also give him the morning star.'* Do you know what the morning star is? It is something that shines even when the sun is shining. We are told that in heaven there will be no sun because the glory of God and of the Lamb will replace the sun and be brighter than the sun, but the morning star means that some people will shine even in the presence of the glory of God — some stars do, the morning star shines as well as the sun. Jesus is showing that if you will keep yourself clear of all this compromise and stand, and hold fast for what you have that is true, then one day you will shine, even in the presence of God. It is a wonderful promise.

Sardis (3:1ff.)

Thirty miles south-east of Thyatira is the town of Sardis, and here in this town we see something which I would like to describe in terms of Edinburgh castle. You may have been to Edinburgh, or at least seen pictures of Edinburgh, even if you have not been to Sardis, built as it is on that massive outcrop of volcanic upthrust so that it seems impregnable. You can get up to that rock in Edinburgh from the east, up the Royal Mile, but on the other sides it drops away in sheer cliffs. Well, Sardis was built more than five hundred years before Christ on top of such an outcrop; it was impregnable. There are three things that I would like to say about this town: it was self-sufficient, it was self-confident and it was self-indulgent — we know this from the history. It was an extremely wealthy place. Even the river that ran round the foot of the hill had gold dust in it, and king Croesus and his treasures were to be found in Sardis. The first modern money was minted here in Sardis. It was here that money came to take far too big a place in what became a very affluent society. The burglars of Asia Minor used to come to Sardis at night, and if you lived there you had bars on your windows. There was so much wealth, it was self-sufficient — they did not need any help at all. Even when an earthquake destroyed the city they rebuilt it out of their own pockets within about eighteen months.

Secondly, it was a self-confident city. Sitting on top of the rock with only one road into the city, they could defend it with a dozen soldiers. They were safe — or so they thought. Twice in history, before this letter was written, they had been taken, each time the same way. The dates were 549 BC and 218 BC. This is what happened. The enemy troops came up and they surrounded the city, and the sentries up on the ramparts saw them, but only on one side did the sentries watch carefully where the road came up. On the other sides the sentries took it easy and just glanced down at them. One sentry on the steep side dropped his helmet and it rolled down the cliff and lodged on a ledge halfway down. He climbed down a path on the cliff which he knew, to get the helmet, and climbed back up. The enemy below, watching him go down and up, said, 'There must be a path there which we can't see. We'll wait until dark and we'll climb up', and they did, and they took the city. That is exactly how Edinburgh castle was taken. Three hundred years later another enemy force came up to Sardis, and they were watching and, lo and behold, this seems unbelievable, a sentry dropped his helmet and they saw it, realised there must be a path and climbed up by night —and they took the city. This was a city that failed to watch, and they were self-confident and thought they were secure. And Jesus says to the church in Sardis, '. . . *if you do not wake up, I will come like a thief, and you will not know at what time I will come to you.*' How appropriate a message.

They were not only self-sufficient and self-confident they were self-indulgent. Being an affluent society they were flabby, they lived for pleasure and leisure rather than work. In fact, one writer said it was a city of amateur dance band leaders and shopkeepers, which just about sums it up. Alas, churches often reflect the town in which they are, and the church was affluent and idle and was not watchful. By the way, shortly after this was written, or about a hundred years later, the pastor of the church in Sardis, a man called Mileto, was the first man ever to write a book about the book of Revelation, which is very interesting. The first commentary on this book that we have came from Sardis.

It was a fashionable church, it was full, it was busy, it was live. Everybody said of this church, what a live church! Crowds of people, big collections, loads of things going on, that was Sardis, and it had the best reputation of any of those seven churches. If you had asked people who knew them all which was the best church, they would have said: you go to Sardis, see how many people they get, you should hear what the collection is!

'You have a reputation for being alive, but you are dead.' Jesus' opinion of them was the opposite of everybody else's. The most important opinion about your church and my church is not what anybody else says but what Jesus says. We could not care less what other people say, we could not care more what he thinks. The church at Sardis was full, it was fashionable, it was wealthy —and spiritually it was a graveyard. They had the form of godliness but not the power. They worshipped, but not in Spirit and in truth; they honoured God with their lips, but not with their lives; they professed to be Christians yet they did not possess Christ. For this reason they were in a most dangerous spiritual condition. I would think that this letter was more devastating to the church than the earthquake had been to the city, and I wonder whether they ever again spoke to the preacher who read it to them!

Even though the church was filled with nominal Christians, fashionable churchgoers, the letter is not all gloom and despondency. The church roll that we keep on earth may not correspond to our Lord's church roll. He says: *'Yet you have a few people in Sardis who have not soiled their clothes. They will walk with me, dressed in white, for they are worthy. He who overcomes will, like them, be dressed in white. I will never blot out his name from the book of life, but will acknowledge his name before my Father and his angels.'* No matter how spiritually dead a church may be, you will discover that Christ has a few names in it, and they stick it out and they go on faithfully trying to retrieve the situation. This is marvellous. I have found it again and again to be true. Sometimes I have been invited to speak at a church where one has felt, on going in, that there was an atmosphere of spiritual death, and that if the Word of God lasted more than twenty minutes there would be an uproar! Yet afterwards maybe just one or two have come and said, 'What a feast of God's Word' — and you knew that somebody there loved the Lord. This is true of all churches, I think: no matter where you go, you will find somebody who loves Christ. That a few in Sardis had not *soiled their clothes* does not mean that Jesus is bothered about what you wear when you come to church. The garments he refers to are the inner garments which you wear on your heart, not on your body — the garments of holiness in the Lord. I suspect there were some good things in that church. In many churches there is a little prayer meeting, just a handful of people still praying and reading scripture.

This letter to Sardis has a call to do three things. First, *'Remember, therefore, what you have received and heard'* (3:3). There is a need to look to the past. Think of how the church began, with simple, godly people who heard, received, and were saved by grace — before it became a fashionable congregation. Then there is a need to look to the present and repent of what they had become — fashionable; dead: *'obey it, and repent'*. And they were to look to the future: *'if you do not wake up, I will come like a thief, and you will not know at what time I will come to you.'*

It is a stern, strong letter but a church that does not do this, remembering the past, repenting of the present and watching the future, is a church that will die and vanish even though it is full.

He offers three rewards. Fur coats were among the specialities produced in Sardis and they sold well. This was one of the main industries. Jesus was telling the few who had not soiled their clothes and those who would overcome that he would give them new coats — they would be '*dressed in white*'. Secondly, of one who overcomes, he says: '*I will never blot out his name from the book of life*'. You can cross names off earthly church rolls and that may or may not make any difference, but the important thing is to keep on Christ's church roll. He lets those who have not soiled their garments and those who overcome know that he will keep them on his books. Finally, he will ensure that they get recognition one day as his faithful people. '*I will never blot out his name from the book of life, but will acknowledge his name before my Father and his angels.*'

Philadelphia (3:7ff.)

We are having quite an 'American tour', and we are just rushing through these towns. I have never physically been to these towns. I would love to go and see them because there are remains of all of them and you can see the Bible come to life. I am going to tell you something very interesting about Philadelphia when I get to the end of the letter. When you know a bit about the town you know a lot about the church. If you want to understand a church in a town the very first thing you might do is to ask about the character of the place and then ask how far the character of the town has been reflected in the character of the church there. The thing that strikes me first about this letter is that Christ has no complaint. Did that strike you too? There is nothing wrong with this church. Would it not be wonderful to find a church where Christ found nothing wrong? What an ideal to work towards and pray for. The name Philadelphia means 'brotherly love', from two Greek words — love of brother. And it was founded by a ruler called Atillus who loved his brother, and he so loved him that he said, 'I am going to call my new town brotherly love' — that is quite a tribute. In fact William Penn, who was born in Buckinghamshire, copied the idea when he founded Pennsylvania, and he called a city in America 'Philadelphia' for the same reason.

Why was the town built? The answer is that it was literally the gateway to the East. Five separate main roads converge at Philadelphia. Coming from the west, these roads go out into Asia; they go to India and right out into the Far East — to China. Atillus wanted to spread his religion to the whole world, so he said: I am going to establish at that junction my town and I will fill it with my temples so that all the travellers come into my temples and take my religion to the ends of the earth. It was built for a missionary purpose for pagan religion, and therefore it was nicknamed *Little Athens* because it had so many temples, so many gods and so many altars, and if you went through Little Athens or Philadelphia you would see all this religion. Its main export was religion and the other one, funnily enough, was wine, and the main god worshipped was Dionysus, so spirits of both kinds were exported to India and beyond.

One other thing needs to be mentioned. Along the main street was a series of pillars on which were the names of citizens whom the emperor or ruler wanted to honour. Instead of being mentioned in the New Year's Honours List and going up to Buckingham Palace for half a day, you had a pillar put up and your name and the name of the emperor who honoured you were put on it, so you were an honoured citizen.

In this town full of temples and public houses, a town full of pillars, a town that stood at the junction of five arterial roads going out to the ends of the earth, there is a tiny church. I do not know how it got there. I suppose that sooner or later a few Christians came travelling that road and lodged there. I do not know how they found employment, because they would not have accepted work in either the winemaking industry (because it was devoted to the god Dionysus) or in the temples, and I do not know if there was any other employment in 'Little Athens'. I do know that, from time to time, this city was devastated by volcanic eruptions and that the Christians were the first to help others when such disasters came. The whole area was called 'burnt land'. Volcanic ash and lava lay around the city; it was a city of peril and yet it was a city of prosperity because, as you probably know, lava, once it has broken down, turns into volcanic soil which is very good for wine growing grapes, so they gained prosperity even from the peril of the volcanic area in which they lived. They had central heating and hot water piped to the houses from the hot springs that came from the volcanoes around. It was a very different city from Sardis.

These are the words of him who is holy and true. Jesus, who is holy and true, looking at this little church, finds nothing wrong with it. Others will *'acknowledge that I have loved you.'* A holy and true person only loves holiness and truth, so we have a picture of a tiny little church which is itself holy and true. They may be small, with only a few members, they may think they are terribly weak, but Jesus says, *'See, I have placed before you an open door that no-one can shut'* (3:8). I find this exciting. In Revelation 1, Jesus has keys in his hand, keys to unlock death, keys to unlock Hades, but there are more keys on Jesus' bunch of keys than that.

There are keys to open doors — what door is he referring to? There are two doors I think he has in mind. One, the door of salvation, the door into the kingdom of heaven. You will never get in by trying hard to live a good life, no matter how much religion you have; you can batter at the door with all your good works. Jesus has the key, and he is the door.

This little church is learning that, though they may feel small, he has opened the door into the kingdom of heaven for them. But I do not think that is entirely what he means. I think he means the door of service, the door of missionary outreach, because he not only has the keys of heaven, he has the keys of earth, and once he has opened a door no-one can shut it, and once he has shut it no-one can open it.

We are very much concerned today that country after country is closing to the gospel. Let us not be so busy looking at the closed doors that we neglect to see the open doors. When the door to missionary work for Baptist missionaries from this country closed in Angola it opened in Brazil, and although we think that men may be closing and opening doors I believe that somebody else has the keys, and that if Jesus wants his servants in a particular country *he* opens the doors. Paul, writing from prison, says that the word of God is not bound. There is before me an open door. If God wants his word in a country he opens a door and no government can shut it. And if God sees fit to shut a door no amount of church pushing will open it. Therefore every church ought to ask: What door is

God opening just now to us? —and not spend all their time looking at the door that is shutting. When an opportunity comes we should take it; when the door shuts we should move on.

Here then is a tiny church, and Jesus says, *'I have placed before you an open door'*. What does he mean? He means every one of those five roads out of the city. There are travellers coming in, and he is teaching them to take them into their homes, give them a night's lodging and send them on with the gospel, not the religion of Dionysus. I wonder whether you have heard the story of Gladys Aylward, who died in 1970. Remember how she opened the Inn of the Sixth Happiness on a trade route in China. And how traders came in suspiciously, but because she told them goodnight stories when they went to bed they came in increasing numbers, and the stories were the stories of Jesus, which they loved because they had never heard them before. She was doing precisely what Philadelphia was called to — an open door. The door of China was subsequently officially closed to Gladys Aylward. What did she do? Did she spend her time fretting? No. She just moved to every other open door, in Formosa, all over the world. She did not start grumbling and say, well, that door shut, that's my work over, I'm finished, I'll just retire — far from it. She was still seizing open doors, almost to her dying day. She was not bothered about shut doors, she saw the Lord opening doors, and when he opened a door in she went. The Inn of the Sixth Happiness was what Philadelphia was called to do. *'See, I have placed before you an open door that no-one can shut.'* You can send Christianity to the ends of the earth. It is a thrilling story.

The church in Philadelphia was a busy little church. Jesus said, *'I know your deeds'*. They had this glorious opportunity and even though verse 8 might suggest to us that they were small in number and had little influence, that does not matter. A little church with a big faith in God can do much more than a big church with a little faith in God. So their incapacity for witness was not a handicap. Jesus moves on to talk about their fidelity. This is the secret of successful service for the Lord. We are not called to be successful, we are called to be faithful. I thank God that in every church I have been in there has been a nucleus of people you never needed to worry about; you never needed to ask, will they be there next Sunday or won't they? They were there. You never needed to say, 'I wonder if they are still doing that job that they took on' — they were doing it. It is thrilling when you find people who are faithful, who hold fast his name and do not deny it, so that you do not need to worry about them. Christians should be worried about those outside, they should not have to worry about each other; we should have all of our resources available to seize the open door rather than worrying about keeping each other up to it.

Now verse 9 tells us that they were having trouble from the Jews in town. There was also a Jewish synagogue which held that they were the true assembly of God, not the fellowship of Christian believers. Jesus makes it clear that they are wrong. *'I will make them come and fall down at your feet and acknowledge that I have loved you.'* There is trouble coming, but the church there has endured patiently, so Jesus says, *'I will also keep you from the hour of trial'*. When trouble comes, everything depends on whether before it came we kept holding onto Christ. If we held onto Christ before, then when trouble comes he will hang on to us. It is my sad lot from time to time to visit people in serious trouble who are like a ship in a storm trying to get an anchor down; if only they had put the anchor down before the storm hit them they would have been secure.

Jesus says in v. 11, *'Hold on to what you have so that no-one will take your crown.'* He has a crown waiting for them which they will wear, but he wants them to wear it, not lose it. They are not to forfeit this by denying him. If one day he can place that crown on their heads as those who overcame, he will do two things for them. First, *'Him who overcomes I will make a pillar in the temple of my God.'* We talk about a pillar of the church. Winston Churchill called himself a 'flying buttress' — he supported it from the outside — but pillars inside the church are much more valuable. Jesus says of the person who overcomes, *'I will write on him the name of my God and the name of the city of my God, the new Jerusalem . . .'* and, *'I will also write on him my new name.'* In a city with all those pillars down the main street, what a tremendous thrill. You may have walked through Westminster Abbey and seen the monuments to great Englishmen — a museum of history. Have you ever thought that the names inscribed on the pillars in the new Jerusalem will include the names of very ordinary people who would never get their names into somewhere like Westminster Abbey? As there is the tomb of the unknown warrior in Westminster Abbey there will be 'pillars' of known warriors, still living, honoured by the Lord in the new Jerusalem.

Finally, here is the exciting thing. Having spoken of the coming *hour of trial*, Jesus said to the believers in Philadelphia, *'Hold on . . . .'* When the religion of Islam, bursting out of Arabia, swept through the Middle East, establishing itself by sword, it swept most churches away out of North Africa. It spread round through what we now call Turkey and in town after town the whole place went Muslim. It carried on, right to the gates of Vienna in Europe, but there was one church that held on — Philadelphia. I can tell you now that some two thousand years after this letter was written Philadelphia (now called Alasehir) is a town which still has a strong Christian presence in the middle of Muslim Turkey. Jesus said, *'Hold on to what you have . . . '* —and I find it terribly exciting to think that there is one church in existence today that can read the letter to the church at Philadelphia and say that is us, we have hung on. I do not know how often they read it or how often the preacher preaches on it, but it must be thrilling to have a part of the Bible that mentions you and your name particularly, Philadelphia.

So they hung on, and I hope and pray that they will hang on until the Lord does come back. They have managed it for around two thousand years, and if they go on they will still be there, and I hope and pray that we in our respective churches hang on too, and that, however long or short may be the time before our Lord comes, when he comes he, the one who is holy and true, may find no fault in us but may say, 'I have loved you'.

Laodicea (3:14 ff.)

This is the last of the letters to the seven churches in Asia. None of them is addressed to our churches so we do not quite get the biting edge which must have come to those who originally read these letters. They did not go separately to seven different churches, they all went to all of them, so they all heard the worst about the church down the road, and they must have dreaded the one that was addressed to them. Some of these letters had nothing to say concerning anything wrong with the church, some of them had nothing about anything right. And the last letter, to Laodicea, cannot find a single good thing to say about the church —not one! I daresay this letter is the best known letter of all of them, partly because one text in it has been preached upon more often than any other text in the book of Revelation, '*Here I am! I stand at the door and knock*', and I am afraid usually that text has been used as if it were addressed to those who were not Christians. It is not, it is addressed to those who are. The tragedy of that text is that Jesus was having a job getting into Christian lives and into the church; the door at which he was knocking was the door of the church, not that of some poor cannibal or criminal, or some other dreadful sinner. That puts the text back into its context, and just as a jewel is best set off in the right setting, so that text when it is put back into its context becomes a most searching message.

Let me tell you a little about Laodicea. Here we are right round the circle: Ephesus, Smyrna, Pergamum, Thyatira, Sardis, Philadelphia, last stop Laodicea, and there is nothing left of that town today —nothing at all. It is a melancholy wasteland with a few ruins, testimony to a town that had nothing but money. The reason it had money was that it was a trading centre. Many Jews lived there: there were at least five thousand Jewish residents by the time Christ was born, and a hundred years later there would be even more. The main commodity which was bought and sold, for which the town was noted, was cloth — raven black cloth made of fine wool from soft wool sheep. The man who founded Laodicea had named it after his wife. It was the banking centre of Asia Minor and if someone in Asia Minor told you he worked in the city, he invariably meant Laodicea.

In the year AD 60 — that is just thirty years before this letter was written — the entire town was destroyed in an earthquake, but they had so much money that they just set to and re-built it. There were more millionaires (in terms of the wealth of those days) in Laodicea than anywhere else. Because there was a lot of wealth, there were a lot of beggars there. If you walked down the streets of Laodicea you saw wretched, pitiable, blind, ragged people, and they were hoping to catch a few crumbs from the millionaires as they passed by. Extremes of wealth and poverty.

Not only was it a place of wealth, it was a place of health. It had a good climate, but apart from that there were healing centres. There was a medical school, there was a good hospital. They even worshipped the god *Men*, the 'god of healing', in this place. In particular it was famous for its drugs and medicines, and there was one medicine which was sold in powder form which you ground up and then made a paste with water and put on your eyes, a special eye salve or ointment for which Laodicea was renowned. Jesus knew about that, which is why he mentions it in the letter.

All these local details make the letter live. But there is one local detail that makes the whole thing really have meaning, and it is this. A few miles away across the plain, in the volcanic area nearer to Philadelphia, there were hot geysers or springs which came up through the earth, and on the way collected a lot of mineral salts in the water, emerging from the earth piping hot, and from the geyser or spring it wound its way across the plain and finally dropped down to the sea. Although it came out of the earth hot, by the time it got to the sea it was cold, but by the time it passed through Laodicea it was lukewarm — it was neither hot nor cold. And if you know anything about water like this, you will know that you cannot drink it when it is lukewarm. I experienced this out in Aden. The water came up through a natural deposit of Epsom salts and there were only two ways to drink it — either straight from the artesian well, piping hot, burning your tongue so that you could not taste it, or after putting it in the fridge, then drinking it when it was very cold; but you could not drink it in a tepid state, it acted as an emetic, and if you are a medical person you will know what I mean.

Jesus writes a letter to the church in this town — a place concerned mainly with wealth and health, and the welfare state is largely concerned with those two things. Here was a miniature welfare state in the sense that the two main desires of life were for wealth and health, or health and wealth, whichever order you put them in, and you went to Laodicea if you wanted to be possessed of both these apparent blessings. In that place was a church, and Jesus, looking at the church with those blazing and penetrating eyes of his, could not see a thing in the church that he could even commend, and it is so unlike Jesus not to begin by finding at least some good point in the church.

He begins his letter by reminding them that he is infallible. I believe in the infallibility of Jesus. I would feel terribly insecure if my religion was not founded on something or someone infallible because I would never know whether I was right or wrong in my faith. But there are three things about himself that Jesus begins with. First, *'These are the words of the Amen'*. Some people when they talk to you are always using the word *honestly* — have you noticed that? It is as if they are terribly afraid that you will not believe that it is honest. If you were speaking in Greek and wanted to use that kind of expression, but in a very much more serious way, you would say, 'amen, amen', which means 'verily, verily', 'surely, surely', 'you can rely on everything I say' — Jesus is the only absolutely reliable person there ever was.

Secondly Jesus describes himself as, *'the faithful and true witness'*. How many of your friends can you really trust to tell you the absolute truth about yourself? It is good to have some who will do this for you, to whom you could go and say, 'Just tell me the real truth about myself' — assuming you have the courage to go and ask that. How many of your friends would hedge at that point, would try and evade the issue, or would come straight out and say, 'Well, since you ask me . . . .' When Jesus describes himself as, *'the faithful and true witness'* he means that he will tell you the truth about yourself. He will not flatter you, nor will he denigrate you, he will tell you exactly what he sees, and that will be the 'amen', the truth. This church was living on a false reputation, and that town was filled with flattery and falsehood as people complimented each other — not because they were telling the truth, but because they were seeking social advantage. Then he terms himself *the ruler of God's creation*. This does not mean, as the Jehovah's Witnesses have tried to make it mean, that Christ was created. The word used here means *source*. Jesus can tell you the truth because all things were made through him, and he knows all about it.

We move on to verses 15 – 17, the most terrible indictment of any church. We notice there is no trace of persecution of this church, there is no trace of paganism in this church or in this letter, there is no trace of idolatry or heresy or immorality in this letter. None of the other things that he saw in other churches is here. What then does he see that is so terrible? The answer is *indifference* and that is worse than anything else. Nothing kills a church spiritually more quickly than indifference. *Laodicean* became an adjective in the English language — it has just about died out now but you will still find it in some dictionaries — and it means to be lukewarm, half-hearted, happy-go-lucky; easy come, easy go.

Let us look at this indifference a bit more. Reading this letter, I get a picture of a respectable church in which you rarely heard the word *hallelujah*, and if you did it would be from someone insensitive to the frozen glances of everybody else sitting around them. Here is a church that would count that as enthusiasm, a church that would think it rather *infra dig* to let go once in a while and to get excited about the Christian faith; a church that has settled down to a fairly smug, complacent, 'go to church, do your bit, go home, finish' — that kind of thing. And Jesus says some extraordinary things. He says, *'I know your deeds, that you are neither cold nor hot. I wish you were either one or the other!'* He would rather you were hot — and I am sure he would rather that best of all. There is a place for hot gospelling, provided the temperature is raised by the right thing, but Jesus would rather they were cold than lukewarm. This is not how the world thinks, and this is not how many churches think. Many churches would rather have some lukewarm members there than some cold members not there, but I think I understand why Jesus would rather they were cold and right out than coming to church and lukewarm. Because it is the greatest insult to Christ to be lukewarm; far better to be right out and cold than to play about with important things like this and to be half-hearted in a matter of life and death. Not only is it an insult and dishonouring to Christ, it wrecks the church. You would be far better out of it than lukewarm — you are holding it back. It is also despicable to the world. The world respects a Christian who can get enthusiastic about his faith; the world despises a Christian who is just half-hearted. Jesus, remembering the stream that ran through Laodicea, says, *'I am about to spit you out of my mouth'*. It seems that lukewarm people make him sick. Are there some things in your life that make you sick —make your throat choke up? Is there something that disgusts you so much that you just want to go out and be sick? Jesus feels that way about a lukewarm church. Indifference! I hear many people talking with disgust about the indifference in the world to Christ; Christ is far more concerned with indifference in the church, for that is what causes indifference in the world. Believe me, where a church is on fire, people will be hot and cold towards the church; they will be violently antagonistic or violently pro, but they will not remain lukewarm outside if the church is not lukewarm inside. They will take up attitudes, and a church that is hot will make a world cold or hot, it will not make for a lukewarm world. And if there is indifference outside, the first question we have to ask is this: is it because there is indifference inside?

The second thing that Jesus saw was their *independence* —I need nothing. Why was that? The answer is they were so rich they thought they had everything; they thought they could buy everything; they thought they needed nothing, and that is why the prayer meeting in the church was dead, because you only have a live prayer meeting in a church when people in the church feel they need God. If you do not feel you need God, you do not go to the prayer meeting. If the church does not feel the need every week of God's grace they do not get on their knees for it. So you can judge a church's independence by its prayer life. An independent church that needs nothing would only keep up prayer as an outward form, but a church that needs God is on its knees praying. Therefore I judge that in the church at Laodicea people came to church out of a sense of patronage rather than a sense of privilege. Patronage says, 'I support that church'; privilege says, 'that church supports me'. To patronise a church is a dreadful attitude, as if God needs you — God can do perfectly well without you. It is a privilege to belong to a church; we do not patronise it, we do not support it, we count it a privilege to draw grace and love from Christ through the fellowship. Independence!

The third thing he saw was *ignorance*. They were utterly ignorant about their real position. In this country many were saddened, appalled and touched by pictures we saw from Sudan. We thought: 'wretched, poor, pitiable'. But it may well be that God in heaven looks down on our affluent West and says, 'wretched, poor, pitiable'. We have been looking at physical things; God looks at spiritual things, too. He looked at Laodicea and saw wealthy people; he saw complacent people there in church and said, *"You say, 'I am rich; I have acquired wealth and do not need a thing.' But you do not realise that you are wretched, pitiful, poor, blind and naked."* They were in a state of profound and terrible ignorance; they honestly did not know what they were really like. So he instructs them. Instead of this independence or self-sufficiency, they are to come to him and then he will give them three things. Firstly, true 'gold'. You do not need to have a lot of money to be rich. True gold is something that comes to you through fire, through refining experiences of suffering and hardship, through the troubles and dangers of life — and really wealthy people are not those who have a big bank balance but those who have been refined by God. Secondly, if they will come to God he will give them 'white clothes' to wear. They were fond of the black garments that were produced there in Laodicea. God would give them white ones. Black was not the colour he wanted them to wear on their hearts, he wanted them to wear white. In a wealthy city like this, where they would be terribly concerned about the outward garments that they were going to buy and wear to meet in church, this was obviously significant. Thirdly, he would give them ointment for their eyes, so that they may see. He is not referring to physical eyes — that is not their blindness — he is referring to the blindness of the soul that is blinded by the god of this world and cannot see itself. Sometimes, when you come to church, suddenly in the sermon you see yourself as you really are — it is not a very nice sight — and it is as though Jesus is putting the spittle on your eyes and saying: go and wash. It is as if Jesus is saying to you that he is putting salve on your eyes, the eyes of your soul, so that you can see yourself and see him.

In verse 19 he makes his intention absolutely clear, that he is going to deal with this church, he is not going to let them go on like this. He says, *'Those whom I love I rebuke and discipline.'* As a child, I once lived next door to a family where the parents were terribly modern in their psychology and never punished their children. I used to envy those children. They painted the cat and the garage doors and got away with it, and this was 'expression' and, 'Ah, we must develop this artistic talent . . . ' —whereas we had very much more painful interviews after doing such things! In my silly, childish way, I thought that their parents must love them much more than mine loved me. I know better now, and I know what that kind of 'love' does to children. If you really love someone, you reprove and chasten — it is part of love. So Jesus will deal with them because he loves them. He calls on them to *be earnest, and repent.* The higher you go in society, the more earnest zeal — enthusiasm

— is frowned upon. That is what was happening at Laodicea. It is good to have a 'hallelujah' now and again, it is good to express ourselves, it is good to be enthusiastic and be warm, hot, excited; let people think we are drunk — they have thought that ever since the day of Pentecost, and they are quite wrong, but let us at least show some enthusiasm for the Lord. Repent then, and get on fire.

Now, after all that, comes verse 20. How does a church that has got as wealthy and healthy and indifferent as this get back onto the right track? It gets back when one man lets Jesus into his life. I remember hearing a story about a church in New York which was far from being colour blind, and somebody who was black tried to get into that church and was shown the door and sat down wearily on the steps outside — so the story goes — and looked up and noticed a tall figure with long hair and a white robe. The figure said, 'What's the matter?' The man said, 'I have been trying to get into that church and they won't let me in', and the figure said, 'Well, I have been trying to get in too, and they won't let me in either' — and the figure vanished.

Do you see the point? *'Here I am! I stand at the door and knock.'* Jesus is letting us see that he cannot get into a church like this, he is outside, knocking at the door. Knocking at the doors of churches! It is an astonishing picture, but I dare believe it is still true that there are churches where you will find Jesus outside on the steps, knocking, wanting to come in. You will notice that he says, *'If anyone hears my voice and opens the door . . . .'* So anybody could just get up and let him in. Even one man in such a church who is letting Jesus right into his life is going to help to change that church and get it out of indifference. It is amazing how one person who really is on fire for Christ can do wonders in a church. One loving heart sets another on fire. Here is the answer to a church that has become complacent because it is too wealthy and too 'healthy' and too indifferent.

Why don't people answer the door when he knocks? I have a copy of the familiar little picture, *The Light of the World*, by Holman Hunt. It was never meant to illustrate Revelation 3:20, but since most people use it to do so, I shall. There are two copies in existence, one in London the other in Oxford. When I first saw that picture I was terribly curious to know what it was like on the other side of that door — it somehow awakens it. I was thrilled to discover another picture. I do not know whether you have seen the other one, but it shows the inside of the door and Christ coming in. I like that sequel, because it seems to round it off into a 'happily ever after' picture. It depicts the same doorway, from the inside. Here is a King knocking at a door to get in. Isn't that remarkable?

I visited a young offenders' institution a long time ago, to talk to the boys. The governor was a marvellous man, and one of the boys told me this: 'We all respect the guv, I'll tell you why: he always knocks at our room before he comes in.' Is that not tremendous? He respected the boys — however bad they had been, he was not going to force himself in. He respected them, and he knew that he must have their co-operation. That helps us to see why Jesus, King of kings, who could walk straight through locked doors, stands and knocks — because he is not going to force anybody, in any church, to have him in; he is just going to knock. He will come in if you let him, but he will not come in otherwise.

During the war a housewife in the east end of London was dusting her home after a particularly bad raid. She heard a knock at her front door and went to open it. Queen Mary was standing there on the doorstep, and the woman was in her curlers and in her apron! You can imagine the shock she got when Queen Mary wanted to come in and see people as they were the night after the raid! If the King of kings is at the door knocking, why do people not let him in? I can tell you some of the reasons, because sometimes I knock at doors and do not get in.

I will tell you three of the reasons I have found as to why some people do not open doors. One is that they are too absorbed in other things. Sometimes you can hear the television blasting away. They may say afterwards, 'I am so sorry I didn't hear you. Thank you for putting your card in; I'm sorry I didn't open the door.' You can be too absorbed, and a church and Christians in it can be so absorbed in many meetings and all kinds of busyness that they just do not hear the knock.

Secondly, some people are too afraid to open the door. Hugh Redwood, in one of his books *God in the Slums*, tells how he heard of a poor woman in a block of flats who had nothing to eat and he took a parcel of goodies for her. He knocked at the door and he went on knocking, he heard movement inside but she never opened the door, so he left the parcel and he went back a week later. This time he saw her down in the yard and said, 'I called last week but I couldn't get a reply.' She replied, 'Oh, was it you? I am so sorry, I thought it was the rent collector and I hadn't got the rent.' There are some people who are afraid to let Jesus in because they think he is coming to demand something of them. What fools they are! He is coming to offer.

The third reason I have found is that they are too ashamed to let him in. 'Oh dear me, fancy, I am all in a state, I am spring cleaning.' I do not know why people think that mine is an ideal home with everything in place — perhaps they haven't seen it! No reflection on my wife, it is my study that is the worst! But sometimes we are a bit ashamed to let people in — 'Oh dear me, look who it is' — pulling the lace curtain aside — 'and us in a state like this.' Sometimes people hear the knock of Christ and he says, 'Let me into your life' and they say, 'No, I can't let you in while I am in this state, I am in too much of a mess', not knowing that he is the best person to clear up the mess.

I was once walking through the Nottinghamshire lanes with a dear Christian, a burly chap in his thirties called Bill Tate — everybody loved him. I asked him, 'How did you become a Christian?' He replied, 'One day a few of us, a gang of lads, went along to the local chapel to have a bit of a lark and the preacher was preaching on Revelation 3:20. We really made fun of that preacher; walking home, we were taking the Micky out of all that he had said. And I said to all the other boys, "Well, if I let him in, he wouldn't get much of a supper in my life", and they all laughed.' But he could not forget it. He went home and he thought like this: no, he wouldn't get much of a supper, he wouldn't get anything, I have nothing to give him, there is nothing to lay before him, my pantry is empty — and Bill Tate asked him to come in. Jesus said, *'If anyone hears my voice and opens the door, I will come in and eat with him, and he with me.'* So we will give something to each other. I will give him a feed and he will give me one. It will be mutual. He will feed on what I have, I will feed on what he has, but we will sit down and share what we have. That is the picture, and our Lord is still knocking at people's lives. He is not going to batter his way into any church, and if a church does not want

Jesus he is not going to be there. If anyone hears his voice and opens the door to him, that is going to change the church, and that is going to alter the whole Laodicean situation.

Finally, what does he offer as his incentive? *'To him who overcomes, I will give the right to sit with me on my throne'.* There was a gardener in Buckinghamshire in the late 60s who one day received a letter from a lawyer telling him that he was now the Earl of Buckinghamshire! Can you imagine that happening? He could hardly believe it. The newspaper reporters came along to take his photograph. Well, Jesus can grant a place with himself. From rags to riches, because that is what you are in at the moment — rags; from poverty to wealth, because that is what you really are at the moment, poor, and you will be rich. Even though you think you are at the top of the ladder, you are not, you are at the bottom, but he can put you at the top. That is the incentive. The real beggars in Laodicea were the people who had nothing but money, and Jesus came to make them rich. They needed to let Jesus in, and to overcome.

Did Laodicea listen to this letter? Did they do anything about it? No. It appears that nobody in that church let Jesus in. There is no future history of that church, there are no traditions, no legends, nothing has come down to us. If you go to the town today there is not even a trace of the church, not one.

My last word to you must be that if we do not let Jesus into our churches then, quite frankly, they are finished. However healthy and wealthy we may look, we really are poor, wretched, blind and naked, and we need to come to Christ.

HEAVEN UNVEILED
Revelation 4

Between chapters 3 and 4 John has been in an ordinary state of mind. Lying in his prison cell, chained to the wall, he has been thinking over all that he has already seen and heard. He has seen the Lord Jesus, he has received seven messages for seven churches. He might have wondered if that was to be the end of the revelation, but it was only a beginning. As he lay there, suddenly the vision begins again, and in the Spirit the cell vanishes, his chains vanish, and he sees an open door; on earth he can see only a locked door closed upon him, locking him in prison, but in heaven an open door. And through the open door he looks into a world he has never seen before. It is a vision that is so amazing he can hardly put it into words. And here we have artistry in words — he is painting a picture. Do not get lost in the details, get the whole picture. This is a marvellous piece of art, and he is trying to convey to us the feel of what he saw through the door. The voice he had heard before — the voice of Jesus — is going to speak to him again and tell him things.

It is at this point that the book of Revelation becomes much more difficult. We shall come back to familiar ground when we get to the later chapters, but the middle section is certainly strong meat — it requires concentration, it requires meditation.

I once talked to a Pakistani student in Paris who was studying theology and church history. I asked him, 'Do you find the studies difficult in another language?' He replied, 'Well, not really, because the lecturers never tell me anything I don't know.' I said, 'Well, that is marvellous, how did you find all this out?' He said, 'By meditation. You in the West don't know how to meditate and then think about it for two to three hours — that's how I knew.' So, just to check up on him, I asked the lecturers, 'Is he really as knowledgeable as he thinks?' The lecturer said, 'We have to give him 99 out of 100 in his exams. We would like to have given him 100%, but this just could not be. No-one is perfect.' Meditation! You will not grasp the central part of the book of Revelation unless you are prepared to sit and read it and think — just to meditate until you also leave earth, and in the Spirit can see these things.

Why is it so much more difficult from this point onwards? The first reason is that it is stretching our imagination beyond the things that we know. It is telling us of things we have never even seen. We have seen nothing like this anywhere else, and it is not easy to imagine things you have never seen. There are four ways in which our imaginations are stretched. First of all, the scene now moves from earth to heaven. I could not show you any photographs from now on; I cannot show you real places or talk about people on earth. We are in heaven now and that is another world, and most people do not even believe it exists, but it does. However, it is so different that our imaginations are stretched. Not only do we leave earth behind, we leave human beings behind, and we see thousands of angels, but many people do not even think about angels — they do not believe they exist. The first Russian astronaut, when he came back to earth, said that he did not see any angels up there — but they saw him, and I wanted to write and tell him that, though he would not have believed it.

Secondly, we not only move from earth to heaven, we move from the present to the future, and it is always more difficult to imagine the future than it is to imagine the present or the past. We cannot imagine what life will be like thirty years from now; it will be unimaginable, quite different.

Thirdly, we also move from the sinful to the holy, and that stretches our imagination. We know what it is like to be sinful, we do not know what it is like to be holy. This is a different world — think what it is to be somewhere perfectly clean, to have a city in which there is no need for anyone to sweep the streets; this is a different, clean world, and it is difficult to imagine — especially in these days of increasing pollution down here — what it is like to go into a clean, holy world.

Fourthly, we move from the human world to the divine world. We now look at things through God's eyes, not man's eyes. We do not look up any more, we look down. This is a new perspective for us because when we think of heaven we tend to look up. But here, in the next few chapters, it is as though we are up on a throne and we are looking way down and seeing the earth and the universe below us; it is a different perspective — although perhaps space travel and the images which we see from that can give us a similar perspective.

Not only does this section stretch our imagination but it stimulates our worship. I do not know of any passage in the Bible like chapters 4 and 5 of Revelation to help me to worship, to give me a big view of God, which is what the Bible means by magnifying the Lord — getting a bigger view of God, using a magnifying glass for your faith and seeing God is much greater than you thought he was. It is no coincidence that a number of hymns have been based on these two chapters; and you will notice they include at least five hymns of praise. This section of Revelation has made people want to sing:

Holy, holy, holy! Lord God Almighty!
Early in the morning our song shall rise to thee;

and,

Come, let us join our cheerful songs
With angels round the throne,
Ten thousand thousand are their tongues,
but all their joys are one

(see chapters 4 and 5 respectively), as well as many other, more recent, praise songs. The two fundamental themes of all worship are these: we praise God for creating us, and Christ for redeeming us.

The first thing John notices when he looks through the door is a throne. It is marvellous to enter the throne room. I once walked through the rooms of the Palace of Versailles, the Hall of Mirrors, and saw those fabulous decorations right through that magnificent building. But, after I had walked through many rooms, I reached one room which was smaller than the rest, and felt that I had reached the heart of the palace. It was the throne room, and there, lifted up on a dais, was a golden throne. I imagined Louis XIV sitting there issuing his commands — the centre of the French empire, here was the throne room, and great though the other rooms were, and some of them were grander, here was where the power lay, even if the glory was spread out, and this is where the orders were given. Now John, looking through the door, sees a throne and he realises he is looking at the throne room — the control room — of the whole universe, from which every order is issued to every part of the created order. It was from this throne that the stars were told to go into orbit and our earth was flung into space; it was from this throne that everything which came to be was created. One almost feels one should go on one's knees at this point. This is the throne from which we take our orders every day; this is the throne to which we pray.

In a constitutional monarchy it is not easy to get the flavour of the word *throne*. We live in a country in which the Queen has very little power — gradually it is being taken from the throne. We forget two things about a throne in a traditional kingdom. First, the throne is the highest authority in the land and can issue any order to any person. Second, the throne is the highest court in the land to which the highest appeal is made for judgement. Therefore, we get an impression from the word *throne* of a place of power and a place of judgement; a place from which orders are issued and to which appeals are made. This is what the word *throne* means — it comes nineteen times in these two chapters. We are in the royal palace.

As I read these chapters my mind keeps going back to Psalms, particularly Psalms 96 – 99, which are all about the Lord reigning. He has set his throne in the heavens; he judges the earth — this is what is conveyed here. And this is clearly a throne of judgement because there is lightning and thunder, destructive forces as well as being beautiful. I have a little book which has thirty precious stones laid out in it — they are not worth much but they are just small examples of some of the stones. I read this book at the same time as I read the book of Revelation. I look at some of these glinting colours and I try to imagine the throne. For example, here the throne is said to be made like jasper and carnelian, which are both bright red, and emerald, which is a beautiful translucent green; and I try to imagine these flashing colours of red and green — the beauty of it all. I saw some beauty in the Palace of Versailles, but nothing to touch this. This is the precious throne of God. And there is a calmness about it because, stretching out as far as the eye can see, in front of it is a glassy sea. Have you ever stood looking out over the ocean on a still morning with not a breath of wind, when it is just like glass? That is the picture. There is a serenity about the throne of God, it is not disturbed. A serenity — lightning and thunder, yes, but the glassy sea, a combination of power and peace, of serenity and sovereignty, which together tell us that God is King and is on the throne.

These are the colours of refracted light. God is light, and if we could look at God we would be blinded. Our eyes are not enough to take in his glory. Blinding light refracted into the colours of the rainbow. A rainbow round the throne. John is just piling up colours and images to convey the beauty of it all. Whether it was a literal rainbow or literally precious stones does not matter. In fact it says that the one who sat on the throne, had the *appearance of* jasper; the rainbow is described as *resembling* an emerald. John is telling us that this is the nearest thing on earth to what he saw, and we must leave it there, we may just take the nearest things that we can and imagine them multiplied by infinity.

He then sees that round the main throne are twenty-four other thrones. There has been much speculation about the twenty-four beings on these thrones; some have thought that they are the twelve apostles and the twelve sons of Jacob — the Old and the New Testament represented around the throne. There may well be some connection in the number, but the description of these twelve creatures, beings, elders around the throne is clearly that of angels, and here again we are in a different world. Many of us never think about angels — we have left them behind with fairies at the bottom of our garden! And I am afraid that when we were children we thought of angels and fairies in the same kind of terms and grew up to dismiss both, but let us remember that man is not the only intelligent being in the universe, there are thousands upon thousands of angels all doing different things for God in the universe; some day you will see them, you might even see them now — you could even have one knock at your door and entertain one unawares as some people have done, but one day we shall see them and know them.

Here then are twenty-four angels. Who are they? They are God's 'privy council'. That is the thought which is conveyed. For in the kingdoms of the ancient world the king sat on his throne, and then on seats around him sat his privy council — his private council who were there to apply his orders, to issue and execute what he said had to be done. It is interesting that in the Old Testament we are told that the temple and the tabernacle had to be a copy, a little model built and modelled upon the heavenly court, and in the tabernacle they had to have twenty-four courses, or rotas, of priests, they had to have twenty-four prophets and twenty-four Levite porters, as much as to say that is what God has, you must reflect this on earth.

Now we turn to the more puzzling feature. Around the throne are four living creatures. Here we have some very strange creatures. Some people have seen in these four creatures symbols of nature. Later they did become the symbols of the four winds, and indeed the four chief constellations, and some have therefore seen them as animals representing nature before God. I am afraid I cannot go along with this because, once again, the things said about these creatures are attributes of angels. Here are four different angels and the clue to their meaning is to be found in Ezekiel chapter 10. If you know the Old Testament you will understand the New. And in Ezekiel 10 we have four living creatures: a man, a lion, an ox, and an eagle; we have a throne; we have fire; we have many eyes, and a rainbow — so clearly it is the same picture. But in Ezekiel 10 we are told what they are — they are *cherubim*. I am afraid that word is going to mislead us. We think of little babies with wings, very busy on St Valentine's Day, and little cherubs floating around. I am afraid that is the opposite of what cherubim are. There are two groups of angels before God to carry out his will: *cherubim* and *seraphim*. These two groups have different functions. The seraphim carry out God's orders of mercy, but the cherubim carry out his orders of judgement. That is why when someone is to be forgiven it is the seraphim who convey God's mercy. Do you remember Isaiah in the temple? He saw God (*holy, holy, holy*), and God was going to forgive his iniquity, his dirty speech, and then flew one of the seraphim from the altar and touched his lips and said, '. . . *your guilt is taken away and your sin atoned for.*' But in the Garden of Eden when Adam and Eve were shut out of the Garden it was the cherubim who were told to keep them out; they bring God's judgement.

Here we have four living creatures, four angels, to carry out God's justice from the throne. Just as the Queen has the Privy Council, and she has her magistrates and Justices of the Peace and High Court judges, so the throne of God has its 'privy council', twenty-four elders, and it has its high judges — four living creatures. The pictures given of them are meant to convey to us their character. They have the intelligence of a man, they have the strength of a lion, they have the service of an ox, they have the swiftness of an eagle; they have perception, so they have many eyes; they have speed, so they have six wings, but all this conveys an impression of judges under God who are efficient in their task. I suppose that modern art and psychedelic pop art help us to appreciate some of the things that are conveyed here, because here is a message which is not being conveyed in literal, down to earth, blunt language but in vivid pictures. It was this that in fact the artist was trying to convey (I am not sure that he succeeded) in the gigantic tapestry in Coventry Cathedral. If you study that, then you will see his attempt to convey this picture. I think it is almost impossible to convey it in picture form, it can only be done in words, but he was trying.

Then comes the chorus. There is certainly going to be a lot of music in heaven —you will be in the choir in heaven; we will have perfect voices. There will not be a choirmaster, we shall sing a new song. We will not need training, we shall be singing praise spontaneously.

I want to tell you about a little experience I had. I heard an ordinary working man who obviously had no voice for singing. I once heard him singing in the Spirit, and I have never heard anything so beautiful in my life. An instrument would have ruined the music. A minister friend and I sat and listened to this, and it was like a bell ringing out over the fields on a clear, frosty morning. The music consisted of about five notes, just up and down, beautiful singing. My minister friend gripped my arm and said, 'Listen, that is perfect Hebrew.' I did not know a lot of Hebrew then, so I asked, 'Will you translate it for me?' He said, 'It is about the peace of God flooding into our souls.' I listened to that singing of this man who was not a singer, in which words and music were being given directly by the Spirit, and I knew how we would sing in glory. I knew that we would all be given words and music to sing together in perfect harmony, with no practice needed, just pouring out our praise, and I knew what was happening here. Day and night they never cease to sing, always singing glory to God. The creatures sing about what God *is* and the elders sing about what God *does*, and these are the two great themes about God. If we are going to praise him, we must praise him for what he is and what he does. They praise him for *what* he is. He is pure [*Holy, holy, holy*]; he is powerful [*is the Lord God Almighty*]; and he is permanent, always there [*who was, and is, and is to come.*] You can say that about no-one else, there is no-one else in the whole of the universe who is absolutely pure, absolutely powerful and always there.

No wonder this helps us to worship. The elders sing about what God does and they say he is *worthy*. Do you know what the meaning of the word 'worship' is? It means 'worthship'. Every time you go into church your worship tells anybody who watches how much God is worth to you. If you sing half-heartedly and look around and just sing bits of the hymn, that is how much God is worth to you; if you look in your purse for the smallest coin and put a little tip in the collection plate, that is how much God is worth to you. Do you realise what an awe-inspiring thing we are doing when we worship? We are saying, 'That is what you are worth to us.' If we are looking at our watches and thinking, 'Dear me, it is going on long, I must get home' — that is how much God is worth to you. How much is he worth to you — of your time, of your attention, of your song, of your concentrated thought and prayer? We are declaring his worth-ship when we worship; we are saying, 'God, we want to sing our very best, we are singing to you. You are worthy!' We worship — that is what it means. And they say,

> '*You are worthy, our Lord and God,*
> *to receive glory and honour and power . . . .*'

Any human being might become proud if given such glory. I looked at the paintings of Louis XIV in that Palace of Versailles and saw a proud face, a man who thought of himself as divine —you could see it in every line of his face: pride. The glory, the honour and the power he had were too much for him. He was not worthy, he could not handle it. Nobody on earth can handle such glory and honour and power. But there is One —because of his work in creation, everything he made, and because it was by his will that they existed. The will of God is the final factor in everything that exists. The will of God is behind everything in the universe, and this chapter is written here to convey to us this sense: the universe is not the result of chance but of choice; the universe is not in man's hands, it is in God's hands; it is his will alone that allows anything to happen that does happen.

THE LION WAS A RAM
Revelation 5

There is a scroll in the hand of God: God's sealed orders for the universe. Within that scroll, as we shall see, are God's orders for the end of human history, to banish evil, to destroy a civilisation that is godless, that he might build a new universe — it is all in that scroll. And nobody up to this point, no human being on earth, knew how history would finally conclude; nobody knew whether the world would end with a bang or a whimper, whether good would triumph, or evil. The scroll was sealed, but it seemed there was nobody able to open it.

What does that mean? When that scroll is opened, the judgements of God will come upon godless men, and it seemed nobody was worthy to do that. Why not? Because the one to open it had to have been tempted as men have been tempted, and to have conquered. In other words, one of God's principles of justice is this: no-one will judge men unless they have been under the same pressures that those men have faced, and come through victorious. That is a wonderful principle. It means that the judge will be one who understands fully the pressure and remained holy. Seeing this, John realises that there is going to be a terrible issue in God's plan. If there were no-one worthy to judge, then evil would go on for ever. The world would be spoiled for ever. Somebody must be found who is qualified. As John weeps out of frustration that God's plan is going to be held up, one of the elders turns to him and says, *'Do not weep! See, the Lion of the tribe of Judah, the Root of David, has triumphed. He is able to open the scroll and its seven seals.'*

Jesus is the one person who is fit to judge the world. He is worthy because he has been tempted, he has faced sin, he has been on earth, he has been through what men go through, and he has conquered it — he is fit to do it. The phrases *Lion of the tribe of Judah* and *the Root of David* are both phrases from the Old Testament, phrases which the Jews of old used to look forward to the coming Saviour in Christ. If you know your Old Testament you will know the flavour and the meaning of these.

Now comes the great surprise. John looks all around for a lion and he cannot see one. The Lion of the tribe of Judah — he is going to do it. There is one of the four creatures that looks like a lion, but that is not the one. Looking everywhere, he spots an animal he has not seen before, and it is a Lamb. Here, in a sense, is the most amazing contradiction, that Jesus is a Lion and a Lamb together. You see that in his life on earth. The Jesus who could take little children on his knee and bless them could whip money-changers out of the temple. There are very few people on earth that can be a lion and a lamb, perfectly balanced. I know some who are lions, and I wish they could be lambs sometimes, I know some who are lambs and I wish they could be lions sometimes, but to be a lion and a lamb is perfect — wonderful. Facing sinners to be a lamb, facing sin to be a lion, this is the perfect combination. We talk about March coming in like a lion and going out like a lamb, or vice versa, because we say it cannot be both, but Jesus is both. Having said that, may I also add that by the word *Lamb* the Bible does not mean to convey a little woolly, cuddly thing; the picture conveyed to you by a lamb is of those little things gambolling in the fields in the spring, but that is not what is signified here. The word Lamb here is a mature word that means really a ram with horns, a full grown ram, and I sometimes think it would be better, and give a balanced picture of Jesus, if we translated the word *Lamb* by *Ram* — behold the *Ram* of God, that gets across. To be the *Lamb* is not to be weak and small and helpless, it is to be strong and yet gentle. The Ram seen here has seven horns — strength; seven eyes — discernment; the eyes of Jesus were always discerning. He could look at a person and see right through them. Seven eyes, seven horns — here is a tremendous picture.

And as soon as he is seen, the elders and the living creatures cannot stop singing. The first time that we come across harps is here, and with the harps are bowls of incense. These, again, are symbols. I do not know if we shall use literal harps in heaven. If we do, I am quite sure that we will be able to play them naturally. The harps and the bowls stand for the praises and the prayers of the saints. In other words, when you see Jesus the right response is prayer and praise. When you catch a glimpse of the Ram of God, the Lion who is a Lamb, then there are only two appropriate things to do. One is to praise him and the other is to pray to him. So we are told of the prayers and praises of the saints. Do you notice that the elders are holding up the golden bowls full of incense to Christ, and that these are the prayers of the saints? Do you realise that if we really pray now, our prayers are in one of those bowls? Here is the incense which God does like; there is a kind of incense that he does not want, but the incense he does want is the rising prayers of people on earth, borne in bowls to the throne of grace. It is a picture. We cannot think literally of a bowl full of prayers. Here are the prayers of the saints on earth being presented to the Lamb.

What are they praising? Two things. First of all that he has *purchased* [or ransomed] men. The word means to buy and set free. I once heard of a missionary in a part of the world where slavery still applied. I got this story personally, so I am quite sure about it. One day, walking through the market place, the missionary saw the slaves for sale, and spotted an old man being sold. He had been separated from his family and he was going to be sold to be taken away in chains to another country. The missionary was terribly upset about this so he went to the bank and drew out all his money, which was not much, took that money straight back to the market place, and he bought that old man then set him free. He said, 'Go back to your family.'

There is a lovely sequel to that. The man came back to the missionary and said, 'Will you let me be your servant now?' The missionary replied, 'I didn't buy you for that.' 'No,' the freed man said, 'I want to serve you.' 'Well,' the missionary answered, 'you can leave anytime you want.' He said, 'I don't want to leave, I want to stay with you,' and he stayed on with that missionary. Now that is what Christ did for us, he ransomed us, he paid the price, he set us free — no wonder we want to praise and pray. We were in chains, and Jesus came and he ransomed men, and the price he paid was blood, not silver or gold. We were redeemed with the precious blood of Jesus Christ. What a price! 'There was no other good enough to pay the price of sin, he only could unlock the gate of heaven and let us in.'

> *'You are worthy to take the scroll*
> *and to open its seals,*
> *because you were slain,*
> *and with your blood you purchased men*
> *for God . . . .'*

The Lord has done everything possible to save men before

judging them. Far from being a callous, cruel judge who wants to destroy men and blot them out, Jesus gave his own blood to save them from the judgement — he is worthy. Here is someone who wanted to release prisoners, and he is the one who is going to open the scroll.

Now the song moves on and it is taken up by many angels. When we are singing, the angels are singing with us. We cannot hear them, but God can, and that is all that matters. Do you know that if one person in a congregation comes to Christ and finds him as their Saviour, the angels will be singing? I have the authority of Jesus for that. Do you know that every child has an angel watching over it, to see how that child is treated? Every ill-treatment and every wrong teaching given to a child is reported back. Their angels see the face of the Father in heaven. We are surrounded by angels and they are singing. It is a pity that, in English versions of the Bible, translators have missed out a most important word in verse 12, on which a hymn was based, the little word *the*. It should be read: 'Worthy is the Lamb who was slain to receive *the* power and *the* wealth — in other words, all that there is. Christ alone is worthy of all the money in the universe, all the power in the universe — and that is how they sing. Finally, this chorus swells and it is as if the conductor is drawing in new groups of the choir. He starts with just the elders and the creatures, then the angels come in, now he brings in every creature in heaven and on earth and under the earth — they all join, and the whole universe joins in the hymn, and we have the sound of a grand 'Amen', which is a lovely thing. I know that by tradition we may say it quietly, but how it helps worship if a congregation can give the sound of a great 'Amen'. If you really mean a prayer, if you really do praise God, what is the matter with saying 'Amen' aloud?

Are you going to be embarrassed? God is not going to be embarrassed, and that is who you came to speak to. Can you imagine how loud this 'Amen' was? *The four living creatures said, "Amen", and the elders fell down and worshipped.*

Let me go back to the first recorded sermon of Jesus on earth. It was in his own home town before his own relatives, which is not easy. He read the prophet Isaiah and he said, *'The Spirit of the Lord is on me'* and then he spoke of the deliverance to the captive, the bringing of sight to the blind, setting at liberty those who are bruised. He finished, *'to proclaim the year of the Lord's favour',* and then he stopped right in the middle of a sentence and sat down. If he had read the next phrase it would have been *and the day of vengeance of our God.* Many people have mistakenly thought that Jesus did not believe in the vengeance of God — he did — but, you see, it was not the time to read that sentence. When he came to earth the first time it was to proclaim the acceptable year, which means the year in which God will accept anybody, but when he comes again he will come to open the seals of the scroll, the vengeance of God, upon a world that has been evil and turned sour and bad. We will study the seven seals, as he broke each one, and what it revealed of the end of human history. It is an awful picture. It is Christ who is doing it, and we need to remember that. But let us hold fast this thought: though Christ is going to bring history to an end, though Christ is going to destroy the civilisation in which we live, it is the same Christ who did everything he could to save people first. It is Christ whose body was broken and whose blood was shed, that men might never come to this day of vengeance. It is the Christ who bled that we might live — it is that same Jesus Christ. Nobody else is worthy to take the scroll and open it. We remember that at his first coming he came to bring mercy and peace, and we rejoice, and praise him for it.

* * * * *

We are moving into the middle of the wood and the middle of the wood is always the darkest place. But never mind, keep walking with me and you will see daylight before long, and we will come out of the wood into the glory of the new heaven and the new earth. But we are moving into the darkest place. We are here told about the future, the end of the world, and exactly what is going to happen to our world before it all ends.

HISTORY'S COUNTDOWN BEGINS
Revelation 6 – 8:5

There is within the human heart a strange contradiction — everybody wants to know the future, yet in a sense nobody wants to know the future. Provided it is good news we would like to hear it; if it is going to be bad news we would rather not. Therefore, horoscope writers know perfectly well they have got to keep the emphasis on good news — something might just happen next Tuesday that is good for you. And if they think something bad is going to happen they put it in the form of a very mild warning — not to take the bus, or something. This is their way, and they have to give out good news or they could never sell horoscopes. If they really knew the truth and were able to sell that, there are many people who would not want to know. They are hoping for some shred of comfort that some day perhaps their ship will come in.

The truth is that only God really knows the future. God knows everything that is going to happen as well as everything that has happened. Furthermore, Christ has revealed to us as much of the future as we need to know. There are many things that I do not know about the future that I would love to ask, but I do not know because he has not told me, and obviously what he has not told me is better for me not to know, but in the book of Revelation we are told enough about the future and the end of the world to know what is coming and to know what the newspaper headlines will be some day.

Some people are profoundly disturbed by this. May I say right at the beginning that these things were not written to terrify anyone, they were written to Christians to comfort them, and if these things have the result of causing fear then it would straightaway indicate that a person was not right with God as they ought to be. For those right with God this unveiling of the future, terrible though it is, is a comfort, because when you know the worst you can face it much better; when you know the worst that can happen, you can face the future calmly. So often when somebody is suffering from an incurable disease the family engage in a conspiracy of silence which creates an artificial atmosphere in the whole home. I have had some experience of seeing this kind of domestic situation, perhaps as many as most, with the exception of the medical profession — and I have discovered how amazingly people can cope when they know the worst, better than with the unknown, better than with the imagined thing. While a person was left in the dark and did not know what would happen, then they were afraid and worried, but when they knew the worst, a peace came and they adjusted to it.

That is why, on the night before he died, Jesus told his disciples some pretty dreadful things about the future that they would have to face, and then, having told them that the Holy Spirit would come, said, *'Do not let your hearts be troubled.'*

In the mercy of God, he has told us the worst about the future so that when these things happen we should not be disturbed.

I was standing watching a computer with a fellow Christian and he said, 'Doesn't the book of Revelation come alive as you look at this computer?' I said, 'How does it? What's the connection?' He replied, 'We are told in the book of Revelation that there will come a day when unless people have the right number they won't be able to shop or do other things. 666 is the number given here, but can't you see it when we are all locked into a computer, when we do all our shopping by a credit card with a number on it, and if you are not allowed to have the number you can see a ready-made social persecution?' He continued, 'We are being governed by numbers now, and if you don't have the number that fits the computer you won't be able to use the tube train, you won't be able to get your credit card, you won't be able to shop. Can't you see it coming?' He was not saying it as though he was worried or fearful, he was just saying it with a kind of calm foreknowledge that said wasn't it merciful of God to tell us about these things?

To sum up these central chapters, there is a period of unprecedented suffering in store for the human race. If we do not like that then we can go away and be ostriches, we can put blinkers on, and in this lovely, pleasant land we can say, 'I don't want to think about these things, it is bad enough seeing it on the television, I'm not going to allow these things into my mind' — that is one attitude. Another attitude is to face the worst, and then look up at God and say, 'God, it is in your hands and you are going to bring us out of the darkness into the sunshine. And even if the worst is to happen in my lifetime I know the best is yet to be.' That is why we have been given this book. If you find these central chapters a little depressing, that is not necessarily a bad thing, provided that depression does not get you down but lifts you up to look at God again, and to realise that he is on the throne.

We begin, then, with the seven seals. We referred to them earlier — a scroll sealed seven times. As Christ himself breaks each seal he lets loose something in the world which will bring about the end of godless civilisation. All God needs to do to wreck civilisation is to take the brakes off. There is enough evil in the world and in the human heart to wreck the society in which we live. The only reason that it is not wrecked at the moment is that God has sealed it and has the brakes on, but when he breaks those seals and lets the forces loose certain things happen.

The seven seals begin with the familiar four horsemen of the apocalypse. If you study art you may know Albrecht Dürer's lithographs, *The Four Horsemen of the Apocalypse*. This has inspired many pictures and artists over the centuries. They are pictures; again, do not press the details but get the picture. These four horsemen stand for four tragedies, galloping into history, let loose upon the human race. The four are logically related: each leads to the next. The first is the rising of a man with lust for world power. It is simply a warrior on a white horse riding out to conquer. I walked round the famous Hall of Battles in the Palace of Versailles, and the wall was covered with paintings which must be twelve feet high and about twenty feet wide, depicting the famous battles of French history — and almost every one of them had a rider on a white horse. There was the rider on his charger looking down on his defeated foes. The meaning is very clear, you do not need to puzzle about it. Here is a picture of a world ruler, a man with ambitions to conquer the globe and reign over it. One of the other things I did was to visit a little clearing in a forest just outside a little town called Compiègne and to look at a railway carriage in which the armistice was signed on November 11th, 1918. On that very spot Adolf Hitler danced for joy when he made them sign an armistice the other way, and there was a man who was riding out for world conquest — he failed, but here in Revelation is a picture of a man who succeeds, on a world scale.

The second picture is of battle and bloodshed. The white horse speaks to us of a conqueror, the red horse speaks to us of blood. We have spoken of the world wars — a bad name for the two biggest conflicts of the previous century. We have not had a 'world war' yet; we have had wars that have had effects throughout the world, but we have not had a world war. Not even all the countries of Europe were engaged in the two so-called world wars. Here, though, is a picture of the first truly world war, and it is a picture of blood, butchery. All God needs to do to have war on earth is to remove peace, that is all, because in the absence of positive peace war is the inevitable result.

The third horse is black, which is the colour of starved flesh and speaks of scarcity and famine. We have other indications that this is what it means — bread being weighed out in scales, rationed. We have a picture of one day's wage buying enough bread for one day for one person, which means that a man works all day and his wage will only buy enough food to keep him going, not his family, and there is not enough to buy any food, any clothes, any shelter or anything else, a picture of inflation when prices and the cost of living rocket as a result of shortage.

Finally, there is a horse that is pale, literally pale green, the colour of flesh without blood, the colour of sickness and death. We are given the stark and terrible fact of a quarter of the world's population dying. There are four very simple pictures which nobody can fail to understand. These are the things that we can expect on a world scale. We have seen them already on a local scale, and that is what makes it so real. We are seeing this exact course in parts of the world now — these things in the same logical order leading inevitably one to the other: military ambition leading to war; war leading to famine and suffering, and that leading to death. All these disasters are foretold not only in the book of Revelation but throughout the

Old Testament, and not only in the Old Testament, but every one of these four things is predicted on the lips of Jesus in every one of the three Gospels Matthew, Mark and Luke. Lest you think the book of Revelation is a kind of contradiction to the Jesus of the Gospels, may I suggest that you read Matthew 24, Mark 13 and Luke 21. There in the Gospels, Jesus predicted what the book of Revelation predicts, and in fact it is the same Christ predicting it here. These are the first four tragedies.

The fifth takes a remarkable turn. Instead of being a disaster coming to the world population, suddenly the fifth seal is a disaster for the church, and this is so often the case; when there is war, when there is trouble, when there is unrest, who gets the blame? Who becomes the scapegoat? The answer is: God's people. It is happening in the world right now. Think it through in the light of the book of Revelation. It happened in the Congo. My sister-in-law and her husband saw it with their own eyes. It happened in Angola. When there is unrest, when there is political disturbance, when things are going wrong, who gets the blame? So often it is the people of God. Here the fifth seal shows a picture of martyrs who in this terrible suffering have lost their lives for their faith. They have become the scapegoat. As Nero blamed the early Christians for burning Rome down when he had set fire to it himself, so in the last days Christians will be blamed for the state of the world. A prayer is heard which to us might sound un-Christian. Those who had been slain ask God to avenge their blood. Is that an un-Christian prayer? Nothing of the sort. They are praying that the God of justice will show that this universe is based on justice. They are asking that God will put wrong right; they are asking that God will deal with wicked men. That is a good prayer, it is not a malicious prayer. It is a prayer to a God of justice, asking him to do what is right. We then read that *each of them was given a white robe, and they were told to wait a little longer, until the number of their fellow-servants and brothers who were to be killed as they had been was completed.* So, amazingly, God was telling them that more martyrs were coming to join them. God knows exactly how many Christians will die for the faith before the end of history, and it already numbers thousands upon thousands. Even this month people have died because they are Christians.

The next seal, the sixth one, introduces a new factor in the situation that we have not seen before. We rely on the regularity of nature, we rely on the fact that the sun will rise tomorrow, and rise it will, but only because God commands it to. We rely on the stars staying in their place, or we could not navigate our planes and ships; we rely on the moon being there, we rely on the regularity of nature; but at the next stage even nature becomes unreliable. We hear today so much about global warming and the upsetting of the course of nature which we are doing as mankind — polluting our seas, rivers and atmosphere, changing our climate, killing the fish and the plants, and this is what we are doing all the time, poisoning our own world. But here we have a picture of a universe that is beginning to shake. Stars falling from their courses, the moon changing colour, the sun eclipsing, the earth quaking, the sky disappearing as if somebody has rolled it up like a piece of parchment, the mountains and islands removed so that the atlases are out of date. Here is a picture of the whole universe breaking up, shaking, doing unusual things, and in that day we are told that everybody will fear God — everybody! They do not now. I do not meet many people who fear God. I talk to some of the older brethren in the ministry, and they tell me that when they began their ministry when somebody was dying they sent for the minister before the person died because the person wanted to be right with God. Now it is the undertaker who sends for the minister afterwards. There was a time when men feared God, and therefore feared death, but they no longer fear either. Yet there will come a day when the whole world which they had thought was so stable and so reliable will shake, and then they will fear God, and they will pray for death rather than face their Maker, and call upon the mountains: fall on us, hide us from the face of God and the face of the Lamb next to him. It is a terrible day. This is a prediction of the future of history. It is at this point that there is a break, a parenthesis to answer the question: what is happening to God's people while these things are taking place?

So we turn to chapter 7 which breaks into the series of the seven seals and gives us the answer to what is happening to God's people. How will they fare during this suffering? The answer is that God will be caring for them and God will not forget them. You will find commentators disagreeing a great deal about who is referred to in this chapter. It is the happy hunting ground of Jehovah's Witnesses and British Israelites alike, and I must say quite simply that, without going into all the different interpretations, I am just going to give you what I can see as simply and clearly as I am able. I see so clearly that the first half of this chapter is about Jews and the second half is about Christians. I am amazed that anybody can see anything different. The first half of the chapter tells us of God's concern for the Jews at the end of history —the twelve tribes whom he called. The second half of the chapter tells us about his concern for believers —Christians. He is going to watch over them while these judgements come.

First of all, he is going to watch over the Jews. God has not finished with the Jews. Those who think God finished with the Jews two thousand years ago have not read their New Testament, they have not read Romans 9 –11. *Did God reject his people? By no means!* How odd of God to choose the Jews, but odder still for those who choose the Jewish God and scorn the Jews! God has not wiped his hands of the Jewish race, they are still his ancient people and that is why one finds oneself so stirred by political events in the Middle East at this time.

What is he going to do? God is quite determined to bring at least a remnant — a part of his ancient people — through these troubles. A message is given to angels which is delivered by *another angel coming up from the east.* He says, '*Do not harm the land or the sea or the trees until we put a seal on the foreheads of the servants of our God.'* It is a very limited number, 144,000 — not many, considering there are over 5.3 million Jews already living in Israel and 14 million in the world as a whole — but God has determined to save some; he will have some of his people in glory with him, and so, when all these troubles are coming on a godless civilisation, God has some of his ancient people sealed.

There has been a lot of debate about where the lost tribes of Israel got to, and the British Israelites think they got to Britain and America, and that is us now — but that just does not bear historical examination. But I will tell you this: no man knows where the lost tribes of Israel are, but God does. God knows the name and address of every Jew in the entire world, and what tribe they come from. A computer could keep that knowledge but God has a greater mind than any computer. God knows the number of hairs on the head of every single individual, and he knows where the Jews are, and he knows how to lay his hands on them. He commands his angels to seal his people; he is determined to have every tribe of his ancient people kept through this suffering. So I expect to see Jews in heaven, I expect to see them in glory because God does not give up his ancient people like that.

The second half of the chapter is about a group of people from *every nation, tribe, people and language*, so clearly it is no longer the Jews who are being talked of here. These are *a great multitude that no-one could count* — but the other is a limited number.

At first John is just awestruck looking at this great concourse of people making their way into glory, who are singing and shouting. They are singing about Christ, the Lamb; they are singing about God who has got them there; and they are waving palm branches. They are wearing white robes — white is the colour of heaven, black is not the colour that Christians wear. General Booth ordered the Salvation Army when he died to wear white, and they wore white arm bands everywhere. I know Christians who deliberately wear white when someone dies, for it is the colour of glory.

We are told that the great multitude are *standing before the throne and in front of the Lamb. They were wearing white robes and were holding palm branches in their hands.* Who are they? Somebody in heaven says to John as he sees this vision, *'who are they, and where did they come from?'* John replies, *'Sir, you know.'* and the elder says, *'These are they who have come out of the great tribulation; they have washed their robes and made them white in the blood of the Lamb.'*

People are constantly coming out of those troubles into glory. When a man is martyred, that sword sends him straight to glory; when a Christian dies of starvation, they are straight into glory. Now I know that people have said this is 'pie in the sky when you die'. I have two answers to that — one of which is a bit naughty — I sometimes say that is better than pain in the pit when you flit! But the more serious answer I have is this: it may be pie in the sky when you die but the real question is whether the pie is real. There is nothing wrong in offering people pie in the sky when they die if it is real. In a world that will have increasing trouble and suffering I think it is wonderful to know that those who come through suffering for Christ are going to have all their tears wiped away, and they are going to have no more scorching sun and thirst and shortage of food. John is being told what is happening so that he can tell others about it.

How did they get out of the troubles into glory? The answer is that red makes white. Blood is normally one of the worst things to get off clothes, but the blood of Jesus makes you whiter than white. I wonder if you really sense the meaning of that. The only way you can ever get clean enough to get to heaven is to be washed in the blood of Jesus Christ. These are they who have washed their robes white in the blood of the Lamb — that is why they are here. There is an idea around that everybody who dies goes to a better place and is at rest and at peace, and that is a lie of the devil, it is not true. Those who have washed their robes and made them white in the blood of the Lamb are going to a better place. And anybody can do that — the invitation is to anybody at all. Therefore we have this wonderful contrast. The picture on earth that we have had is of hunger, thirst, darkness and sorrow. It is a terrible picture, but here is another picture, a picture of no hunger and no thirst. Just to show you that you must not press the details of Revelation too literally, because if you do they contradict each other, get the picture: the Lamb is the Shepherd. You see the wonderful combination of pictures — the Lamb of God who was slain becomes a shepherd and he looks after them. God shelters them, Christ shepherds them — that is the picture of heaven. If you and I live to see these troubles of the seven seals upon earth (which we may well do; with the speed of world events today I could well believe that these things could happen in the next thirty years) and we find ourselves suffering and weeping, then let us just remember this chapter and remember a God who wipes away every tear from our eyes. It is worth going through the trouble to escape to that better world. Is this escapism? No, it is reality. It would be escapism if this were not true, but it is true. And so this great cosmopolitan multitude — God's plan is to have people from every kindred and tribe and tongue in heaven — these cleansed people are comforted.

Let us return to the opened seventh seal at the beginning of chapter eight. There has been the parenthesis of chapter seven to tell us what is happening to God's people in the meanwhile and to let us know that, whether we are on earth or in heaven, we are safe and that God has his hand upon us. Even if we die, even if we are martyred during these troubles, that is alright, we are just joining a great concourse and going into glory. Now the seventh seal. When the Lamb opened the seventh seal *there was silence in heaven for about half an hour.* Heaven is a rather noisy place in the rest of this book, with people singing, shouting, marching around, but here, suddenly, silence. Why? I am told that in those countries where there are tornadoes and cyclones, one of the ways you know that a terrible storm is coming is that everything goes quiet and still, the air seems not to move. If you are wise you go around shuttering your windows; if you are wise you get ready; if you are wise you put the car away; if you are wise you put everything that could be blown away into a safe place. That is what the silence means here, because this silence occurs in a number of the psalms. You will find that every time there is silence in heaven it is before a storm is about to break. What breaks the silence? The prayers of the saints, after half an hour. Can you imagine John seeing all this in a vision? He has been waiting for the seventh seal to be broken, to see what is to come, and there is a long silence, and for half an hour he waits and then the silence is broken, and as he listens the saints are praying. What are they praying? They would have been praying a prayer they have now prayed for some two thousand years — your kingdom come, your will be done, on earth as it is in heaven. And it is in response to their prayer that the final seal is broken.

Do you realise that our prayers change history? A saint on his knees can do more to affect world history than a politician, or a king on a throne, because you are praying to a higher throne, and the prayer of the saints is for the end of world history. Unless you are close to God and see the world as he sees it, I doubt if you would ever pray sincerely for the end of the world, but when you last said in church *your kingdom come* that is what you were praying for. Jesus told us to pray *your kingdom come*, and those prayers of the saints ascending to God precede the final judgement of the evil of earth. The bowl which the angel uses to carry the prayers of the saints to the throne of grace is then filled with fire from the altar and is poured out on the earth. It is a picture again, but it is telling us that our prayer is the most relevant thing for the future of the whole world. God forgive us if when we get on our knees we do not realise we are changing the course of history.

I think two things surprise people when they read these chapters. First, the appalling suffering of man that is yet to be. I do not believe the world is going to get better and better; I do not think we will have peace on earth — not until Jesus gets back. Therefore I am not among those who have this kind of humanistic optimism that somehow we can solve our problems. I do not believe we can. I believe that suffering will grow rather than lessen. That does not excuse me from trying to relieve it. Please do not misunderstand me on that point — Christians must relieve every bit of suffering they can, but I do not believe we shall get on top of this problem. Some people find this a very difficult thing to accept. The other thing they find difficult is that Jesus himself should break those seals — and I understand that, especially if we stay with the kind of picture of Jesus we acquired in childhood, but let us grow up and see Jesus as the one whom God has appointed, not only to save the world but to judge it, the only one worthy to break those seals, the only one who has done everything that needs to be done to save men from the coming judgement; he is the only one who is fit to bring that judgement.

But there are two things, even in this chapter that we have just studied, that bring hope to me. First of all, the purpose of God is sure. God has willed the future and nothing man can do can stop that. God will do everything he says in the book of Revelation. The second thing is this: the people of God are safe. That is the other side to this, for the main emphasis in these two chapters is not on the sufferings of man but on the safety of those who are washed in the blood of Jesus. That is the main thing that I want to leave you with at the end of this section of our study, so that you may draw comfort, and when these things happen your hearts may not be troubled.

. . . AND CONTINUES
Revelation 8:6 – 9:21

The book of Revelation is a very good test as to whether you
believe the Bible to be the Word of God or not. It has a strange
effect. If you are living an easy, comfortable life, this is a book
that you do not like. It shakes you up, it disturbs you inside.
At the time of writing, it can be nice and easy and comfortable
to live in much of Britain. So this disturbs us; we do not like
to think things like this could happen here. On the other hand,
if you are suffering and going through it, this book becomes
a comforting book and a helpful book. The Christians in
China love this book of Revelation, it is the most comforting
book to them. So if we have a reaction against it, this may
be because we do not like to be disturbed. Nevertheless, we
need to read it. It is not an easy book and we are into the most
difficult chapters. We are getting into some very complicated
symbolism — some of which I do not profess to understand.
But one of the things that I have found helpful to understand
these chapters is this: here we are hearing about things that have
never happened before, so it is not surprising that we find it
difficult to understand or imagine these unprecedented events.
So what I ask myself is this: even though I do not understand
the details of some of these disasters, what is the effective
result of them? When you ask that, it becomes utterly plain.
I may not understand these locusts with their weird faces and
hair and tails that sting and so on, but when I ask what is the
result of that (that a third of mankind dies) then I do understand,
it is clear enough. I may not understand this great army of
horsemen and the sulphur and the sapphire and the fire and so

137

forth, but when I ask what the result is I understand the result, which is that even though men suffer appallingly they still do not turn back to God.

Therefore, what I would suggest is hold on in the book of Revelation to what you do understand, and work back from that to what you do not, and you will find that it becomes clearer. Just bear in mind that until these events happen nobody quite knows what they will be like. John is trying to describe for us what is indescribable because it is beyond our experience, but the results are utterly clear. This book was written not to give you an academic exercise in trying to understand all the symbols, it is to tell you what the outcome will be, and if you read the book of Revelation with any attention at all you will be left in no doubt as to what the results of all this are.

Let us turn to these seven trumpets. John sees the end of history as a series of tragedies. There are three series of seven: seven seals, seven trumpets, seven bowls. We ask: how are these series related to each other? Does one series simply follow another? Are they successive, or do all these things happen together? Commentators have argued about these two interpretations. I am going to keep them all happy or make them all unhappy by saying I think it is a bit of both —simultaneous and successive. I notice that in each series there is a gap between number six and number seven, and number seven is never really revealed. In other words, we are led right up to the beginning of number seven then it stops, each time. Seven seals — we are told what the six are and then, just as the seventh is going to be revealed, there is nothing, silence in heaven. It is the same with the trumpets —you get all six, then on the seventh there is silence. The more I look at this the more I see that this is what is happening. There are six seals and then the seventh is broken up into six trumpets and the seventh trumpet is broken up into six bowls. In other words, we see increasing detail. You see a kind of progression because the plagues that the trumpets introduce are shorter and fiercer than the troubles that the seals brought, and the troubles brought by the bowls are even shorter and even fiercer, so that you get six seals, six tragedies spread over a considerable time causing some suffering, but the seventh is divided up into seven separate things — the trumpets — and six of those come one after the other quite quickly, doing a lot of damage, but the seventh is not told us, and the seventh trumpet is split up into seven bowls. In other words, you have an accelerating climax of disaster, and world history is always accelerating, so this fits in. Events happen with increasing speed and severity so that world wars become more and more damaging and there is an escalation of evil. This is the kind of picture, so that you get seven seals, seven trumpets, seven bowls leading up to the peak, and ever more compressed in time.

Now let us look at the trumpets. These trumpets tell me of two things: the justice of God and the mercy of God. You can see the justice, but I wonder if you see the mercy. The justice is clear: these tell us that man cannot get away with it with God, that man who does evil will one day pay for it. You cannot get away from God. As the farmer said, 'God does not settle his accounts every October, but he does settle them.' Let the human race be warned, if we do evil in God's sight we will not get away with it, God will one day bring justice.

But I see the mercy of God in the trumpets. Why? Because trumpets are used as a warning — they are used as a warning of something coming. During the war there was the dreadful wailing of the air raid sirens; it was a mercy we had those sirens because they told us something was coming, they helped us to get ready for it. And in the State of Israel and in other parts of the world, instead of a siren they used a trumpet — the insistent, piercing sound of a trumpet sounding the alarm. You find it in Jeremiah and Ezekiel — you find it right through scripture: blow the trumpet and tell people to get ready. In other words, why does God not just destroy the earth once and be done with it? Why does he spin it out like this? Why, if God is going to destroy evil men, does he not just do it like that and be done with it? The answer is that he wants to save them. He does not want anybody to perish; it is not his will that any should perish; he does not take any pleasure in the death of the wicked. So God gives warning after warning, he is pleading with men. Can you not see that terrible things and utter destruction are coming?

Sometimes I have discovered that men and women look back on a disaster as a mercy. Time and again men have been struck down with a disease, or they have had a bad accident, and looking back they have said, 'It brought me face to face with myself; it gave me a warning that I am not here forever, and God in his mercy gave me another chance.' The trumpets tell of the mercy of God. They may sound to you like terrible things, but God's will is to save people, so he is showing us the kind of thing that is coming. If he destroys a third of mankind, will the other two-thirds at least begin to seek him?

The first four trumpets go together. They are natural disasters in the sense that they are in the physical realm of nature, and they are supernatural disasters in that they are caused by things happening outside nature, from outer space — the universe — and clearly there is some kind of meteorite activity in thought here. There are terrible things: scorched earth, with trees and grass burned up. I wonder if you realise what that means. The study of the balance of nature is called ecology. We are dependent on the plants. They take in our carbon dioxide and breathe out oxygen, we take in their oxygen and breathe out carbon dioxide, and men and the plants live together in one universe, and we help each other. Pretty well all our food depends on the process of life growing in the vegetable realm — look at everything you had for breakfast this morning. Here is something happening, something invading us from outer space, I know not what, I have not seen this happen so I cannot explain it all, but the effect of it I do understand, that a third of the vegetable life of our world is dead. That will profoundly affect the food situation but it will affect our atmosphere as well, and even our climate.

The second thing I am told about is a polluted sea. Again it looks like meteorite activity and it rather looks as if it would be one happening, say in the Pacific Ocean, which would deal with a third of the waters of the world in which we live. And it is not just pollution because it destroys a third of the ships, which would affect world trade, and that again would affect your breakfast! Consider the things that you had for breakfast that came by ship from overseas — your marmalade, your cereal, your tea, your coffee.

The third thing that is mentioned is contaminated fresh water, the fountains as well as the seas, the springs. There is already a shortage of fresh water in parts of the world. Again, I do not know what kind of radiation or pollution will do this, but the result is clear.

Fourthly, there is reduced light, so that we have only a third of the hours of daylight. Way back in 1950 I lived on the Shetland Islands where during the winter the sun rose at about ten o'clock in the morning and set at about three in the afternoon. It was not very nice living through the long winter with reduced daylight. But we did have compensation — during the summer we had no darkness, and you could read a newspaper outdoors at midnight in the middle of the summer! But imagine living in a winter that is like that all the time.

So here are these four disasters. Why do I think them credible and not some fanciful imagination? Two reasons. Many years ago a television programme which drew attention to some amazing facts: it referred to rivers that catch fire, lakes that turn green, eggs without shells and soil that turns to dust, poisons in drinking water and atomic waste causing earthquakes, schools where sport has to be cancelled because the air is so foul. The programme asked if three-quarters of the world's cities will be flooded. Will future generations see the sun? Will we cause a new ice age? Have half a million children died as a result of nuclear testing? That was a programme, a report on pollution, and this list reads like a chapter out of the book of Revelation. The title of the programme was *And on the Eighth Day* — they even had to go to the Bible for the title. Now, if man can do that to our world — and that programme was one of the most frightening there has ever been — without God at all, what can God do? I find this perfectly credible when I consider what man can do to his own universe — to the sea, the water, the air. We are doing it already ourselves. I do not believe that Revelation is talking about what man will do but what God will do, but if man can do it, God can do it, and more.

The other reason this is credible is that God already did it once. Throughout chapter 8 I get a sense that God is again doing what he did in Egypt before the children of Israel came out —those plagues. The plagues were in his mercy, he was warning the Egyptian people to let his people go, making it clear that they were heading for trouble unless they did his will. But they did not listen, and God in his mercy sent one plague after another; they never listened and they lost all their fighting men. These are the first four warnings.

In chapter 9 we go to something severer still — the fifth and sixth. These are described not as warnings but as woes, and that word means curse. They are now targeted directly against man. The other four things are against nature — the sea, the trees, the grass, the atmosphere, the sun, the light. But now God is trying harder still to break through to men, directing two things against them: insects and invasion. I will never forget being in a plague of locusts once, in Kano, northern Nigeria. I stepped off the plane, and half an hour later, at midday, the sun went dark. I thought there was an eclipse of the sun, but it was not, it was a cloud of locusts. I timed them, they were flying at ten miles an hour, and for three-quarters of an hour the sun was blacked out. They were tiny, so you estimate how many millions there were flying over my head — they were bumping into my body then going on. I saw them come down on a tree, and two minutes later they moved on and the tree was dead — not a leaf was left! There were poor Africans trying to beat them off their vegetables, and they could not do it. I have never seen anything like it. You look at an individual locust and it is nothing. I saw some in a little cage — they are nothing, but you see them in a plague and it is one of the most frightening things you could see. You can see all your food going.

But this is not just a plague of ordinary locusts because: *They were told not to harm the grass of the earth or any plant or tree, but only those people who did not have the seal of God on their foreheads.* The one good thing about a natural plague of locusts is that they cannot hurt you, and indeed, in Kano, men were shovelling them up and throwing them out and brushing them up with brooms as they fell exhausted on the ground. They were not afraid of them themselves, but here are locusts that can sting like a scorpion. Do you know, that is the worst pain the human frame can stand without dying? The nerves and the veins are set on fire. And these insects are most unusual. In fact, they are more than insects, they are insects taken over by the devil himself and given his supernatural power because their leader is said to be Apollyon, destroyer, the devil. In other words, the devil can control nature. Here are insects directly under the devil's control and given power to attack men. Do you think this makes men turn to God? Read the Bible, it says they sought death, not God. Is it not amazing that many people would prefer to die than to face their Maker? Of course they do not realise or do not remember that if they do die they do meet their Maker — the one leads to the other, so death is no way out of this. But here are these men and they run around looking for death and they cannot find it.

The next one — number six — is an invasion from the East. This has led many people to think of the Chinese. Two hundred million soldiers invading across the Euphrates, and many interpreters have said this must be China, and certainly China qualifies. But I cannot be dogmatic on that. I want to say that even if these are human beings invading the Middle East they are inspired again by supernatural evil forces. The real enemy is not the Chinese (if that is who is meant), the real enemy is demonic and this warfare is inspired by the devil, not just a human invasion this time. And here we have these horsemen. I do not know what the colours of fire and smoke and sulphur mean, except that it is a pretty destructive army. Again I see what the result is, and it is very clear — a third of mankind killed by this invasion.

Now we come to the saddest verses in the book of Revelation. I think we touch rock bottom in verses 20 and 21. We really are at the lowest, darkest point. In spite of all this, the rest of mankind did not leave either their idolatry or their immorality — in spite of all this! I remember going to visit a man in hospital who was very seriously ill, and the doctors had said his chances were 50/50. He said to me, 'Mr Pawson, if I get better from this I am going to become a Christian, I am going to go to your church . . .' and he gave me a list of things he was going to do, and he did get better and he did not come to church, and he did not turn over a new leaf and he went back to his sin. A year later I was visiting him in the same hospital with the same trouble. And he said, 'Mr Pawson, I really mean it this time, if I get through this, if God will get me through this I will put my life straight, I will do anything.' He did get better and he has not been to church yet. What is there wrong in human nature that we cannot learn our lesson? We are chastised, we suffer and still we do not learn. These two verses tell us that man is a rebellious, stubborn, stupid, proud being and that the human race will not learn, whichever way God tries to teach. It is a sad comment on our human race that even after going through all this they still do not say, 'It could be that God is angry with us.'

We are talking now about the whole of mankind. Whether they have heard the gospel or not, they have all had two things: creation and conscience. Every man and woman in the world has had some experience of these two things, and creation tells us there is a God. His power and his deity, and our conscience, tell us that God is concerned with how we live. Idolatry and immorality are flagrant contradictions of the two revelations that every man has had. No man has an excuse to be an agnostic or an atheist, the creation is there, there must be a great, powerful deity who made it all. A man who cannot see that is deceiving himself — he is holding down the truth, the Bible teaches.

Every man has a conscience — it may not be as developed or as trained in some as in others, but everyone knows that deep down there is a difference between right and wrong. Yet here is mankind, instead of worshipping the God who made the world, worshipping idols that cannot talk, cannot listen and cannot walk, just lumps of wood and stone, bowing down to them, and their magic and their sorcery and their superstition —and placing trust in horoscopes. That is our human race — our scientific era and our superstitious age. We have five out of ten commandments broken. This reads like the Sunday papers: murder, magic, promiscuity, stealing. I discover as I talk to people that they believe stealing is not wrong provided the person you steal from can afford to lose it. In other words, they think that you should not steal from the little grocer around the corner, but from the supermarket; that it does not matter, as they can afford it; it is wrong to take a small sum from a small person but that if it is a big firm then take it if you need it, it is yours. This is what is being described here. Murder, magic, stealing, promiscuity, mixed with a bit of idolatry and magazines about the occult. Many prefer such things, even though God disciplines them, chastises them, warns them of what they are heading for — but still they go on. It is a tragic fact, the impenitence of man.

We are going to turn to chapters 10 and 11 —even shorter

chapters, but they tell us still more about the mercy of God. Somebody could say at this point, 'Why doesn't God speak to men instead of just doing these dreadful things to them?' The answer is that God has not left himself without witness, and he sends people to talk to man, and what happens to the witnesses? What do these people think of someone who comes and tells them what is going to happen? Let us look at chapters 10 and 11 about those who hear God's Word, digest it, and then preach it.

ANGELS AND MARTYRS
Revelation 10 — 11

Again the details may cloud your thinking but let us look at the heart of it. These two chapters tell us two things. God still has people to speak for him, and he still has places where people worship him. That is the message. Even through all these troubles. And you notice that the insects, when they came, could not touch God's people; there was discrimination here. Now we are told there are still people prepared to pray to God and to preach to men — even in these troubles. It means, by the way, that the church is still there on earth — and still preaching and still praising.

In chapter 10 the prophet is first of all shown a new message in the shape of seven thundering voices, and he is about to write that down for us, but God says, *'. . . do not write it down.'* Why? Some people say, 'Well, God has his secrets and he doesn't want us to know everything', but I think the real reason is very simple. God is telling us about what he could do but is not going to do. He has tried every way, but he is not going to do any more. Then comes the phrase *'There will be no more delay!'* The Authorised Version is very misleading saying that there shall be no more time. The word is *delay.* This means let's get on with it. Let us do one more thing — let us try preaching. That is the message of these two chapters. God has shown them what is wrong, now let someone go and tell them what has been happening, and maybe they will listen. Just as when he sent the plagues on Egypt he sent Moses and Aaron to tell the Egyptians what it all meant, now he is going to send this man John. And John, if he had not done this, would not have given us the rest of Revelation — the little scroll here is surely the rest of this book. The literal word translated *little scroll* is *biblion* which is the same as our word *Bible* — a writing, a book. John is told he must eat this and then preach it. And here are the two things that we are called to do with the book of Revelation. God says to John, it will be sweet in your mouth and bitter in your stomach, and the book of Revelation is just that.

I have found that it is wonderful to preach this book and to hear it preached; it is exciting, it is great, it is sweet in the mouth — God's power and purpose unfolding. But when you go home and think about it, a bit of it is bitter. Have you had that experience already? You have probably found it interesting and exciting, but then you have had second thoughts and, as you have digested it, it has become bitter. One person after studying this book said, 'I don't really know whether I want the future to come or not. On the one hand I want it to come to get it all over with and to enter the new kingdom and the new heaven, and on the other hand I don't want this to happen.' It becomes bitter, and indeed if it does not become bitter as you digest it I wonder if you have really eaten it. We are not just to read it and look at it like children looking at a plate of food and pushing it around with their knives and forks, we are to eat it and digest it, but expect it to be bitter. And in fact you must have a heart of stone if you can read this book and not feel how bitter it is, though sweet to the mouth. We like to study it and, while we eat it, it is sweet, but it becomes bitter as we ponder it, yet we must do that. Then, when we have felt both the sweetness and the bitterness of this book, we have got to preach it.

I have heard preaching of this book which had only tasted

the sweetness, and therefore someone was almost gloating over the destruction of the wicked. You cannot preach this book like that. I have known others preach it who simply were bitter about it and had not tasted the sweetness, and therefore they could not either. Only if you have tasted the sweetness of this book and then felt the bitterness of it are you ready to preach it.

Then God says to John, *'You must prophesy again about many peoples, nations, languages and kings.'* I would like to emphasise our responsibility here. Christians are the only people in the world who know how the world is going to end; if we do not tell people they will never know. They will consult their horoscopes, they will buy Old Moore's Almanack, they will study the stars, and they will read the wild predictions of politicians, and their hearts will quake for fear because they know not what is going to happen. Fellow Christians, if we do not eat and preach this book, who will? The tragedy of our day is that there are whole churches where this book is never read and there are Christians whose Bibles still have the pages stuck together in the middle of the book of Revelation, who do not like it and who run from it and stick to little promise boxes to get the nice bits — there is a place for that, but if we do not tell the world how it is all going to end, who will? Eat it, bitter though it may be, and then preach it.

Be quite clear in your mind that the nearer we get to the end, the more we preach it, the more opposition there will be. I am not giving you entertainment and I am not giving you easy, nice, comforting material. The nearer we get to the end of history, the more the witnesses of Jesus are going to be persecuted. Here we have John told to do two things — *measure the temple of God and the altar, and count the worshippers there* (I do not know how he measures, but he is going to do so) — and then he is shown a picture of two witnesses.

There have been many arguments as to where the place is and who the two people are. Let us just get the main message before we get lost in details. The main message is that in spite of everything there is still a place on earth where God's people are worshipping, but it does not need an outer court now because nobody wants to join them. The court of the Gentiles is trampled underfoot. In other words, we have a picture of a church that has stopped growing, a church that does not need to have rooms for outsiders, a church that is the people of God praising, and from that praising community, which is measurable, countable, there come out two preachers who are going to have a last try to convince the world that God is going to judge. Some people have asked whether they are Moses and Elijah. Certainly they are like them in what they do and what they say, but I do not think we can press that — we are not told who they are. Some have said they are Calvin and Luther, but that was because they thought the fifteenth century was the end of the world. Though I do not know who they are, I know that God is ensuring that there are preachers right at the end; and so that people get the message, an adequate testimony, from more than one, it is in the mouth of two witnesses. They have the power to back up their message with miracles and still people do not listen. Finally these two are killed, their bodies are degraded and strung up for people to see and laugh at for days; but God, performing one more mighty miracle, brings them back to life and takes them to glory.

Now, for the first time in these two chapters, we find people terrified of God and giving glory to him. This is the first little breakthrough; you can almost see God trying every way he can to get through to men, and now at last there is a little chink of light. After the earthquake which accompanied the ascension of the two witnesses, *the survivors were terrified and gave glory to the God of heaven.* (We remember that Jesus had witnessed, performed miracles, died, risen and ascended, and the people gave glory to God.)

Now we come to the last section. Look at 11:15−19. It is like a breath of fresh air after all this — terrible though it is, we now have the most wonderful section. The seventh angel blows his trumpet, and instead of a woe, instead of tragedy, instead of something terrible happening, what does he hear? Happy voices first, happy voices giving thanks to God, praising God. Why? Because at last Christ is going to rule the earth and the kingdom of the world becomes the kingdom of our Lord and his Christ, and he shall reign for ever and ever. After reading about all that has happened up to this point, it amazes people that we could give thanks to God. After seeing the tragedies that are coming and being disturbed by them, here we are thanking God. His kingdom is coming to replace the evil kingdoms of the world. Russia is not going to rule the world, China is not going to rule the world, America is not going to rule the world. Who is going to rule the world in the last days? The answer is Jesus, and then the destroyer is destroyed.

Sometimes men and women ask me this: 'Why does God let evil go on? Why doesn't he do something about it?' Then, when you read them the book of Revelation and say, 'He is going to do something about it', they say, 'Oh, I don't want him to do that.' We cannot have it both ways — either he will destroy the destroyer and rule as King, or evil here will go on for ever.

Now the trumpet sounds again, and there were two occasions when the trumpet was used in Israel — as a raid siren and as the 'all clear'. I remember what it was like at the end of an air raid during the war when that wail went again, but we loved it then and were excited. When it went up and down our hearts sank and we scrambled for the cupboard under the stairs or the air raid shelter. But when it went up and stayed up we came out thrilled when it was over — the 'all clear' had been sounded. The seventh trumpet is hailed as the 'all clear'; now the kingdom is coming; now we are nearly at the end, which is in sight. And so they sing — they sing about the nations that raged. God has the last word. We recall Psalm 2 — the nations conspire and plot, the rulers gather against the Lord, but God laughs, and he rebukes them in his anger, and in his wrath he terrifies them. God always has the last word.

Finally, we come to 11:19. Having measured an earthly temple and place of worship, John now sees the real thing of which all earthly temples are a copy. He looks up and he sees a great, marvellous temple. Here is the place where God will be worshipped for ever and ever. There will come a day when all the troubles, wars, famines and plagues of earth will be like a bad dream after you have woken up. All the troubles of which people are reading in their newspapers today will be gone, and we shall be worshipping in another temple. This is where the book of Revelation keeps lifting you, and time and again in the darkest time you are lifted up again into heaven to see, until when we get to chapters 20 and 21 evil is behind us, wars are behind us, famine is behind us, plagues are behind us and there is just the new heaven and the new earth and the glory of the Lord, tears are wiped away and suffering and pain has gone —but tribulation comes before we enter the kingdom. Some people would love a short cut, some people would love me now to jump to chapters 20 and 21 so that we can jump straight into glory, but I am not going to, because Christ's teaching is always that it is through tribulation that you enter glory.

THE WOMAN AND THE DRAGON
Revelation 12

We are now right in the middle of this book and we are in the darkest part of the wood and I think everyone acknowledges that chapter 12 of Revelation is the most difficult one of all to interpret and I am quite sure that my remarks will not wholly satisfy you or answer every question that you have. It is difficult to interpret for a number of reasons.

First of all, our Western minds are so literal that we do not like symbolism, we like a thing to say something in a straightforward manner. Let me give you an illustration. Our typical British attitude does not like Annigoni's portrait of the Queen, on a very simple ground that it does not look like her, whereas what he was trying to do was to give us an insight into certain aspects of her character; he was not trying to take a photograph or he would have used a camera, he was trying to tell us about her loneliness, her severity, her seriousness and a number of other things. Because it was not like the chocolate box painting he did earlier, many have not liked it. Our Western, literal minds want a picture to be exactly the same as the real thing, then we understand it. But if a picture is meant to convey some deeper understanding, by caricature or even distortion, we find it difficult. The pictures given to us in the middle chapters of Revelation are not just straightforward photographs of the future, in a sense they are rather like Annigoni's portrait. They are saying something about the future, and some of the features in the picture are perhaps a little symbolic, and we find it difficult to understand, but I think if you apply yourself to it and think hard about it you will get the message.

Secondly, of course, we are dealing with future events, and the future is always difficult to understand because we have not experienced it yet. If you had tried to convince my great-grandfather that he could have sat by his own fireside and watched the Olympic Games in Beijing he would have said you were mad! He would have said, 'I just cannot understand that, I just cannot imagine it' — and we have the same difficulty with the future revealed here.

Thirdly, many of us are not suffering, and it is those who suffer who understand this book most easily.

Next we are dealing here with supernatural beings — with angels, with the devil — and we live in an age which knows little or nothing of the supernatural, and therefore we tend not to think about angels and the devil; we talk about people, about evil and good, but rarely about angels.

How do we tackle these chapters? We go for things that are clear, things that we do understand. That is the place to begin. If you are facing a lot of things that you do not understand, first try to understand one of the symbols and build on that.

Then secondly, do not get bogged down in details, get the picture of the whole, get the main thrust of the passage. If you are looking at a modern picture, you do not look at each little detail first, you stand back and get the whole impression — what is it all about? For example, with Annigoni's picture, if you look at just some of the little details they are very interesting, but the first thing you should do is stand back and look at the picture and see the loneliness of it. A small figure in a large empty background. He is saying the Queen is a lonely figure, all alone up there on the throne. This is the kind of thing Revelation does. Many people have got too bogged down in the little details before they have stood back and got the main impact of the whole picture.

I do not know whether you got a lot or a little from reading chapter 12. Just to put it into its place in the book, we have had seven seals, seven trumpets and we expect to go on to the final series of seven bowls, but instead chapters 12–13 come in the middle as a kind of parenthesis. We would call it today a flashback. Often in a film there is a flashback to previous events, just to fill the knowledge so that you can understand what will follow, to give you more explanation.

Chapters 12, 13 and 14, of which we are only considering the first two now, are a flashback to the troubles we have already had mentioned in 9–11, but we are now going to be given much fuller detail.

We must ask two questions: first of all, where are the troubles of the world? Where do they begin? Where do they start? For example, take Vietnam. Where did the trouble in Vietnam start? Who was responsible for it? We realise that this local conflict between the North and South Vietnamese was something much bigger. It was a struggle between capitalism and communism, a struggle between East and West, and the local suffering of the people in the Vietnamese villages was the symptom of a much bigger war that was going on. We ask where is the war that is causing all the suffering on earth? The answer is that it is not on earth, it is in heaven. The biggest war in the universe is not anywhere on earth; it was not Vietnam, nor the Middle East; it was not the 1914–1918 nor the 1939–1945 war; the biggest war in the universe is going on in heaven, and our troubles down here are simply the overspill of that mighty conflict, and that is where the real war must be settled. If it is not settled there, then we are going to go on in trouble here.

This is a concept that many find difficult. They do not see that our wars on earth are the result of the war in heaven, and that when that is settled then the beginning of the end of our troubles is in sight.

The next question I want to ask is: how long does this war last? In these chapters we have a number of references to a period of 1,260 days, or 42 months, or three and a half years, or a time, two times and half a time. And this period, given to us in so many different ways, is one single period of three and a half years during which the troubles described here will happen. That is a short time — thank God it is — and Jesus himself said to his disciples that the Lord has shortened the days, so that in fact people will not suffer for too long.

The scene in chapter 12 is in the heavenly dimension rather than the earthly. Therefore there is frequent mention of sun, moon and stars and other heavenly bodies. This gives you the atmosphere of heaven; we are away from the earth. In chapter 13 we will come back to the sand, the sea and the shore — that is down to earth again — but in chapter 12 we are in heaven and we are looking at a conflict. The atmosphere, the main thrust, is a struggle, a war, a conflict between the devil and someone else, in which the devil is defeated. That is the main picture, and as you look at this picture you see the devil trying his best to destroy someone and failing to do so. With that main picture there can be no disagreement.

But now we come to the particular details. There are two portents, or signs, in heaven — a woman and a dragon. We have to ask, who is the dragon? Who is the woman? There is no doubt as to who the dragon is, nobody has any difficulty because we are told he is that ancient serpent, the devil and Satan. If you do not believe in a personal devil you will not make any sense of this book, because the real conflict in this book is between the devil and God, or the devil and Christ. You will not make any sense of our Lord's temptations, or of the cross, or of this last book in the Bible unless you believe in a personal devil. Now you do not need to believe in a little black creature with horns and a forked tail — the Bible never describes him like that — the Bible only says what he is like. He is like a prowling lion, he is like a snake, he is like a serpent, a dragon, he is like all these terrible things. The contrast is with the picture of the Holy Spirit who is like a dove. Which would you rather have around you, a dove fluttering, or a snake creeping up on you, or a prowling lion outside your door? These are pictures, but they convey a feeling, they convey a reaction in us to the picture that is given, and if you want to know what the devil feels like, then if you saw a prowling lion outside your front door that is how you would feel if you met the devil; or if you saw a big snake coming through the grass of your front lawn, that is how you would feel if you were to meet the devil.

We do not meet the devil nearly as often as we think we do, and he gets a lot of blame for things that really are our fault. Never speak as shallowly as this: somebody gets out of bed the wrong side in the morning, they do not get out when they should, they are late, they miss the train for work, they arrive at work too late, they are bad-tempered, they fall out with the boss, and then they dare to come to a Christian fellowship at night and say, 'The devil really got at me this morning.' It was not the devil at all, it was their own fault, it was their own weakness of the flesh, and we must not say a thing is of the devil when it is our fault. On the other hand, when you do meet the devil you know you have, because you feel as if you have met a lion, or a snake, or a dragon. Martin Luther used to throw his inkwell across the study at the devil when he felt his presence — an evil presence, you can almost smell the devil. That is the dragon and his colour is red because he is bloodthirsty; he has seven heads because he is one of those creatures very difficult to kill — chop one off and another one will grow. He has ten horns, which gives you an idea of his powers; he has seven diadems because he is the prince of this world and controls the kingdoms of this world. All these give us the picture.

Now comes the difficult one — who is the woman? I am afraid there are many disagreements about this woman. I can only give you three of the main interpretations and tell you which one makes sense to me, and leave you to choose. The Roman Catholic interpreters see Mary here, as the woman clothed with the sun and the twelve stars on her head and the moon under her feet; and they see the male child as our Lord Jesus; and they interpret this picture of Mary bringing forth Jesus, and the devil waiting to kill him at birth, as indeed he tried to through Herod when the babies at Bethlehem were killed. At first sight that seems a straightforward interpretation, but when you look at what happens to the woman and to the male child in the rest of the chapter it does not fit Jesus or Mary. It is the wrong time because this is at the end of history, and it is the wrong story. It just does not fit, so personally I cannot see that it is Mary.

There is a second group of people who see the woman as a personification of Israel, her children the Jews, and the male child Jesus again, and many Protestants see this in the woman. Once again I find it very difficult to fit the story into any meaningful and logical sequence. The things that happen to the woman and the children just do not seem to fit, and the timing certainly does not.

The third interpretation, and the one that seems to me to make sense, is that the woman is the church. It was John Calvin who said, 'If God is your Father the church is your mother', and there is a very real sense in which the church brings forth children and has more and more offspring — Christians who are born again in the world through God's work in the church.

As soon as you say the woman is the church it begins to make sense all the way through. We are dealing with the end of history and Satan's hatred is of the church — the larger part of which is now in glory in heaven — and he hates the woman and he wants to do something about her. In this case the male child is a personification of the martyrs of the last days — and once you say that, again, everything fits very clearly. The rest of her offspring are the other Christians who are not killed but left in the world. If you take that to be the meaning — the woman being the church, the male child whom she is producing out of her trouble and travail as the martyrs, and the rest of her offspring as the other Christians left in the world — then you can see what the devil is after. The first thing he is after is to stop those martyrs, because martyrs produce more glory to God, and so build the church. And therefore the devil wants to obliterate martyrs, but actually when the church, in her travail, produces them, they ascend straight to glory and they are beyond the devil's reach, and all he is achieving is filling up heaven with his enemies.

That is the picture given. It is a horrible picture of a woman with child in pain, and she has got to produce the child since labour has started, and here is the devil waiting to pounce on the child and destroy and obliterate it because here is a potential rival. The martyrs are martyred, but instead of obliterating them they are in glory and the devil is defeated. That is the picture. So, in the end of the chapter, he turns his wrath against the surviving Christians, and he tackles them in another way, as we will see in chapter 13.

Here, then, is the picture: Satan is in heaven now, not in hell. This again is a fundamental misunderstanding. Most cartoons of the devil show him down there in the flames, sending demons up to earth to do damage. In fact, the opposite is the picture. Everywhere in the Bible, the devil is presented to us as in heaven — he is an angel. In the book of Job he comes back to heaven from earth, to talk to God. When you become a Christian you are in a battle, not with men and women — however much you think you are, you are not, you do not wrestle against flesh and blood but you wrestle against principalities and powers and spiritual hosts of wickedness. Where? In the heavenly places. In other words, the day you get through to heaven is the day that you will get through to the devil as well as God — and if a person tells me they do not believe in the devil and have never experienced his presence I would question whether they have really got through to God. The moment you get through to God in heavenly places, that moment you will be up against the devil in heavenly places — you are into the front line of the battle. You never knew the devil before, because you were not in heavenly places and that is where the devil is.

We now move on to the middle of this chapter. I have dealt largely with the beginning and the end — the devil failing to destroy the martyrs because they ascend to glory, and he cannot do anything more to them then, having killed the body. So he then, at the end of the chapter, turns his attention to earth, and attacks very severely the rest of the Christians. But in between verses 7 to 12 the war in heaven reaches a climax, and a decisive victory and peace comes to heaven. It may be a bit shattering to you to realise that there is war in heaven (or that there will be) and that it will reach this climax. But if you want to know something of this battle then get on your knees and pray and see how much of a battle it becomes. As soon as you pray, you will be entering into the heavenly battle and there will be every possible reason for you not to, and you will find it a battle to pray. New Christians, I warn you that it will be a battle; everything you do in the heavenly places, every time you get in touch with heaven, you are in a struggle and a battle —you are up against forces too great for you unless you allow the Holy Spirit to give you power.

Coventry Cathedral is a controversial building to say the least, but it has some wonderful features — the baptismal window is sheer poetry in stained glass to me. But outside that window, on the wall, you will see a caricature, a sculpture. You see Michael the archangel with a spear, and below him the devil, defeated, cowering. It is a magnificent sculpture; it speaks, and it is taken from Revelation 12. It says to everyone who goes into that cathedral to worship that the devil is already a defeated foe —his days are numbered; Michael is stronger than the devil. In other words, in coming into this church to worship, you are coming into a battle, you are not in church to sit down quietly and enjoy a picnic, you are coming into a battlefield; you will be fighting, even in church, but do not worry, the forces of good are greater than the forces of evil, and that is what the sculpture says as you go in the main door. You do not need a sculpture to say that, but you do need to know that when you come to church you are coming into the front line of a battle. We are seeking to contact heaven and therefore the devil will be contacted too, which is why the devil will do anything to stop you reading the book of Revelation, because it unmasks his devices and it unveils his doom.

How many angels are involved in this battle? The answer is all of them, but two thirds remain loyal to God and one third follow the devil in his revolt and rebellion. On earth we are seeing a lot of rebellions and revolts today — minority groups trying to take power from those who have it. Now this is so often the devil's own work, and he himself is doing the same thing in heaven. He leads a third of the stars of heaven, sweeping them with his tail, bringing them under his authority and using them as an army against the forces of good. But Michael, the archangel, and all the good angels (two-thirds of them) are greater in strength, and the devil is defeated. So there will come a day, some day in the future, when the devil will be turned out of heaven, and all his angels with him, and heaven will at last be a place where there is no discord, no disharmony, no conflict, no struggle that pours out suffering on earth as a result. I do not know if this disturbs you, but it is the truth that heaven is not the most peaceful place at the moment, and that if we were to go and live with the angels today we would go into a place of conflict not a place of peace, and this conflict is described here, but it is over here. Do you know what defeats the devil? Here we have a clear statement: *They overcame him by the blood of the Lamb and by the word of their testimony.* Who? Those who *did not love their lives so much as to shrink from death.* The devil cannot fight the life of a man or a woman who lives for God consistently. He is defeated by the testimony of those who conquered him — by the blood of the Lamb and their testimony. The very best weapon you can ever use against the devil is the word of your testimony; you can say, 'Well, I can't answer all these questions, I cannot explain suffering, I cannot explain the evil in the world, but I do know this: that by the blood of the Lamb my sins were forgiven — that is my testimony. You may be able to tie me in intellectual knots, but I can tell you this: Jesus saved me.' Now that is the thing that conquers the devil, and the war in heaven will be won because there are so many in heaven who have loved not their lives even unto death.

The devil is a liar from the beginning, and a slanderer. He says anything he can to destroy the reputation of God's people. He is the *accuser*. We recall that James says that the tongue is *set on fire by hell*. The devil uses the tongue more than any other part of the body —to say things that are not true about other people. One of his accusations is that people only love God for what they can get out of him. Satan has put abroad the lie that when it comes to the push people will save their own lives rather than acknowledge God. It is a lie, and there have been martyrs every decade for two thousand years. Heaven is packed with people who have loved not their lives even to death, and have died rather than deny the faith. There are people in the world doing that today, and heaven has many such martyrs. Martyrs are more than a match for the slanderer and the deceiver of the whole world. That is what will finally destroy him. When one thinks of the martyrs of our day, some of whom we know about, some of whom we have not heard of, they will ultimately see that Satan is pushed out of heaven. When he is then like a cornered criminal he will vent all his anger on the earth, and chapter 13 tells us what will happen on earth during the period when the devil, frustrated in heaven, decides to attack the rest of the Christians, though not by martyring them, which would just put more of them in heaven. The devil will change his tactics from direct physical persecution. Let us read chapter 13 which will make much more sense to us now.

BEASTLY TAKEOVER
Revelation 13

We are now down to earth again. The devil is subtle and cruel; he is going to use men to suppress the church, in particular two men: a world dictator (a political leader), and a world religious leader. I believe that here we have the clearest picture of what will happen to our world at the end of history.

There will be one world government in the hands of one man and there will be one world religion led by one man. That is what I predict. And that is why I cannot, as a Christian understanding this book, work for a united single world government. However much United Nations workers see this as their hope for the future I dare not work for it, because the nearer that comes the nearer this comes. If we get one world government, then quite frankly it will not be long before it is a single dictatorship. That is why I have reservations about ecumenical dialogue, because the dialogue has already in my day gone far beyond Christian churches talking together. Protestants and Buddhists and Hindus in India have long been in ecumenical dialogue. There is already a world congress of faiths, and I have long received literature in my letterbox asking me to offer prayers in church for one world religion. These things are happening already. We are moving into greater political blocs. I find myself with very mixed feelings about the European Union, but not for the reasons that are commonly brought forward. We are moving into ever greater political blocs heading for world government, and we are also moving into this mixture of religion heading for one religion, and it is of the devil, not of God.

Consider world rule. The beast from the sea, otherwise described in the New Testament as Antichrist, the man of lawlessness, is a dictator on a world scale. We have seen dictators on smaller scales, but this is universal.

Notice six things about him. First, recall that most dictators choose an animal as a symbol, whether a lion or an eagle. Here are his: a leopard, a bear, a lion. It is interesting that all three of those were used as symbols of revolution in the twentieth century.

Second, his diabolical authority. The horns, heads and crowns remind us of the authority we saw the devil had in chapter 12. When the devil offered Jesus all the kingdoms of the world, he was offering Christ the post of Antichrist, but Christ refused it, and one day a man will be offered it and accept it.

Thirdly, his amazing stamina. We have in the mortal wound to one of his heads an attempted assassination, yet he recovers from the wound, and this makes people think he is wonderful and marvellous.

We notice, fourthly, his blasphemous language and name. I would not be surprised if he called himself Jesus. It has long been a popular name in the underworld with those who like to parody the truth.

Fifth, notice his religious persecution. We learn that the only people who will not worship him will be those whose names are written in the Lamb's book of life. Christians are to endure patiently and with faithfulness.

Sixth, there is universal dominion over every tribe, every people, every tongue and every nation. In the name of our Lord, and on the basis of the Word of God, I predict that there will one day be one world dictator over everybody but the

Christians, who will be the only people who will resist. How will he get hold of the rest? The answer is that if you are going to control men you must not only get hold of their bodies and their minds, you must get hold of their souls — and therefore you must have a state religion that you can control.

In the second half of chapter 13, from verse 11 onwards, we see another beast — a religious beast called the false prophet. You see, a totalitarian state cannot keep its hands off religion. It has got to get hold of men's souls.

I notice again six things about the false prophet. First, he has a Christ-like appearance. I envisage a kind of benevolent archbishop who is kindly and nice, whom people falsely assume to have the graciousness of Christ. He has two horns like a lamb. Jesus was the Lamb, and I imagine a false prophet of Christ-like appearance, not an obviously terrible man, but an apparently nice, kindly man who takes the post of minister of religion for the world state, but speaks like a dragon, with deception.

Secondly, notice his established authority. It will be an established religion linked to the world state, and every citizen will have to go through initiation, marrying and burying ceremonies of this world religion.

Thirdly, I also see that, even though he is human, he is treated as if he is divine. Some of the Roman emperors were treated thus.

Fourthly, I see that he will have miraculous power. This false prophet, having told the people to worship the world dictator, now performs miracles. (The devil can perform miracles.) He will make the image of the first beast speak, and will call down fire from heaven.

Fifthly, I notice idolatrous worship. Huge pictures of the

ruler will be everywhere — and images everywhere, to which people bow. If you have seen any pictures out of North Korea, this does not seem strange at all.

Sixthly, the most subtle, cruel form of persecution of Christians is not to be thrown to the lions but severe economic pressure. I do not say this lightly, and I do not want you to think that I mean it as such, but I would find it much easier to go to the lions and get it over with than to see my children starve because they are a Christian's children. I could not face that. I think that if you have children you will appreciate this. Here is economic pressure: it envisages that everybody has to have a number, even to go into a shop. The number given is 666. We need not get involved in all the weird and wonderful explanations of that — people have made that mean Nero, Caesar and I do not know who else. We shall know when this beast comes, we do not need to know now who it is. The point is that unless you have a number on your right hand or forehead you will not be able to shop, you will not be able to buy or sell, you will not be able to go to the job centre to get a job, you will not be able to do anything. Here comes a day when a number is branded that can be seen.

How would you like to live in a world in which you were not allowed to buy food and you could not work? Instead of being thrown to the lions you just had to watch your children waste away. That is what I see here. Thank God he is still on the throne and he has limited it to three and a half years. That is all the time the beast has. Then Christ will return.

Why does God allow the Antichrist even three and a half years? Simply to show men what happens to human history when God is ignored. This world was meant to be the kingdom of God, reigned over by Christ with the Holy Spirit leading religion, and if men choose — as they do and as apparently they want — the devil to have the kingdom and the Antichrist to reign, and the false prophet to lead their religion, then God allows mankind to see just what this leads to — and who can say that is wrong of God?

HARPS AND HARVEST
Revelation 14

The book of Revelation is there in the Bible to tell us how the world is going to end and what lies beyond the end of the world. It is there to tell us accurately what future history will be like — the kind of events we can expect, some or all of which may occur in our own lifetime. Every Christian generation hopes that this will happen soon, so that the new heaven and the new earth can come. The picture of the future it presents is grim, and you may have found it disturbing.

There are two things you can do with facts: you can either close your eyes to them — they are still there, of course, but you are happier because you are not looking at them — or you can face them squarely and ask this question: why should God want to disturb us? Why did he not leave us in ignorance about the terrible trends of future history? Why did he not leave us happy as we were? Why did he put this book in the Bible? Why has this wretched preacher written about this book when there are plenty of other things in the Bible that he could write about that are much nicer? Why should God want to disturb us so much by telling us such grim things about the future? The answer is he wants to get you ready. Far better that you should know the truth and be ready for it. And I find that wherever God disturbs me in the Bible by showing me the truth, he always adds comfort. This is typical of the Lord Jesus Christ. He warned his disciples that in this world they would have trouble, then he immediately said, *'But take heart! I have overcome the world.'* This is so typical of our Lord Jesus that I am convinced the book of Revelation, as it claims, comes direct from Jesus himself. He tells us the worst, then he encourages us.

Chapters 12 and 13 make for grim reading — I know that.

We have seen in those chapters, towards the end of history, a growing tension and conflict between the church and the world. But this conflict is due to a tension between the devil and Christ — a battle which is going on up in heaven but which spills over into the earthly sphere. In chapter 13 we saw that at the end of history Satan will switch his tactics, from direct persecution — killing and putting more and more Christians in heaven as martyrs — to a subtle social pressure which is far more difficult to bear. As the Christians will not take the mark of the beast they will not be allowed to buy or sell, or have employment. In other words, instead of being thrown to the lions, you would just be thrown out of the Job Centre and the supermarket. That is very much more difficult, because it means that normal life becomes impossible. It means that you would only get anything from scraps thrown out. It means that you would be around the dustbins looking for your next meal and it means that you would see your own children starve.

I remember visiting a little village overseas. The Christians there, meeting in their little church, told me this: 'There is only one school within reach of this village, and the authorities of the school will not let Christian children into it. Therefore our children grow up illiterate. We cannot teach them because we never learned how to read and write. And we see all the other children in the neighbourhood being educated, learning how to get a job, how to climb the social ladder, whereas our children are going to be beggars for the rest of their lives.' Yet they still went to church. Knowing how eagerly families in Britain who can afford it get their children into better and better schools, I wonder how many would still be in church if their children could not get any education because their parents were Christians. That is the kind of pressure, and it is a terrible pressure. That is the forecasted prediction of the Word of God concerning the social situation in the last three and a half years of history, and it will be tough.

Now, having told us the worst, chapter 14 shows us many things that will help you to get a balanced view — not to panic, not to fear but to face the future calmly and serenely.

What are those things? Seven different visions or voices in this chapter give us seven facts about the future which you can put on the other pan on the scales, to weigh up against the grim persecution that will come.

What are these facts? The first is a glimpse of the martyrs — a large number of them — 144,000 of them who have been martyred during the time immediately preceding this last trouble. This is not the 144,000 of chapter 7, which clearly referred to Jews, these are Christians, and they are people who have died for their faith. We catch a glimpse of them in heaven. Are they down-hearted? Are they sad that their lives were cut short? No, they are singing their heads off! In other words, what we would count as a tragedy they count as a triumph; what we would count as a terrible end, they see as the beginning. And the first vision that John has, lying there in prison that Sunday morning, is of a great number of people thrilled to be in heaven, almost thanking their persecutors for getting them there early. I wonder if we really feel like that. We tend to congratulate people on getting better from illness and coming back from the gates of death.

I remember Herbert Silverwood, that great evangelist, who went every year to the sands at Yarmouth to preach, and at the end of one week he went paddling in the sea. He could not swim and the beach shelves rather sharply there, so he got out of his depth and into difficulties, and shouted, 'Help!

help!' So the lifeguard dashed in and pulled him out. Then the rescuer said, 'I don't understand you, Mr Silverwood, you have been preaching all week about the joys of heaven, and the first chance you get to go there you are yelling for somebody to pull you back!' Herbert Silverwood was never at a loss for a reply, and he looked down at his swimming trunks and said, 'Ah, but I wanted to go decent!' He told me afterwards that it was a challenge to his own soul. We congratulate people who get better and who escape death, but the martyrs are thrilled to be in glory.

There are three things said about them that qualified them for this particular honour and for the honour of singing a special song composed for them by God and taught to them by the Spirit. The three things are *chastity*, *loyalty* and *integrity*. Now do not get this wrong, they are not there because they remained single. The Bible never says that the single state is higher than the married state, nor does it say that the married state is higher than the single state. Some are called to one and some are called to the other. Jesus himself said that some are called to be single for the sake of the kingdom. Some are called to be married, too. So there is no distinction here between a higher and a lower level, and we cannot base that on the Bible wherever we do get it from. These three qualities which are said to characterise the lives of the 144,000 are the opposite of social life as it will be at the end of history, when marriage will perhaps hardly exist as a relationship, when the family tie for life will be almost an unheard of thing. It is rapidly going now of course, but toward the end of history chastity outside marriage and fidelity inside it will be almost unheard of. But these are people who, in spite of the trends, in spite of the popular fashion, remained pure and chaste.

Secondly, they remained loyal. *They followed the Lamb wherever he goes.* It implies that there will be many who will come to a point where they will say, 'I was prepared to follow Jesus this far, but no farther; I am not going that way, it will cost me too much.' But these had the loyalty which says wherever you go, I will go.

The third thing was *integrity*. In the world, at the end of history, truth will be one of the rarest virtues of all. I glanced again at George Orwell's *1984*. Winston Graham working in the Ministry of Truth, twisting the papers, twisting books, twisting so that you did not know what was true and what was not. Good is bad, and black is white —this was his job, the Ministry of Truth in the totalitarian state. Where the government does not tell the truth the people are not slow in following their example. And this is the kind of future I see, in which you will not be able to trust people. I think one of the most disturbing things about France that I found was a widespread assumption that the other chap is out to do you, and you must look after yourself because nobody else will, and you must expect him to try and deceive you. This is so even into the income tax and the legal world, as I discovered from missionaries who had been honest in legal matters. It shattered me, and yet, if I am going to face the facts, can we point a finger over the Channel? In a day when honesty is gone, these Christians had no lie in their mouths. Here was a group of people who kept chastity, loyalty and integrity, such rare virtues; so they were martyred, but they took those virtues with them.

These are only the *firstfruits*, which means the beginning of the harvest. So John sees this vision — what a comfort — here are people who hung on to those virtues when nobody else did, and there they are singing in glory, and there is a sound *like the roar of rushing waters and like a loud peal of thunder*; it is also *like that of harpists playing their harps*. It does not say they had harps, but it sounded like that. If you can imagine a concert hall full of harps, and Niagara Falls in the background, you have got something like the sound of this new song. That is enough to cheer you up!

Secondly, in verses 6–7, we have a vision of a flying preacher. I can never read verse 6 without thinking of my friend Flight Lieutenant Murray Kendon. During the war he was on coastal work around Britain. He had been out over the Atlantic, and he had succeeded with his crew in destroying a German U-boat, and he was flying back. At first he was elated, ready to report the death of this submarine, and then he began to sober up, and he began to think: here am I, all the skill in my flying hands, and I am using it to destroy and kill; and then he thought — every air force in the world is designed, for all its skill, to do this. Then he had a further thought which he thought was ridiculous at first: why shouldn't we have an air force to do good? He could not get rid of that idea. When he was demobilised, in 1946, he came to London, took a little office there, and he prayed for an aeroplane and he was given one, and the very first time I ever flew in the air was in that little plane, so it was a double thrill — your first flight is always a thrill, but particularly so to be in that little aircraft. From that one aircraft has grown an 'air force'. You may have heard of The Missionary Aviation Fellowship. That was Murray Kendon's baby. It all started because he saw this text: *I saw another angel flying in mid-air, and he had the eternal gospel to proclaim to those who live on the earth . . . .* That text encouraged him to go ahead, and missionaries all over the world have benefitted from the aeroplanes Murray Kendon prayed into his 'air force'.

What does the vision of vv. 6–7 mean? Simply this: that to the very last minute God will give people an opportunity; to the very last trumpet, he will see that the gospel is still being preached. Even during these troubles there will still be an opportunity for men to turn to God, and if men will not preach, then an angel will step in and preach, but the gospel is going to go out. Some people have an odd idea of the gospel — they think that the gospel is 'God is love' and that is all. That is not the gospel of my Bible. The gospel of my Bible begins, *Fear God*. You can love him then, but you fear him first. The eternal gospel the angel preaches begins, *'Fear God'*. Unless you fear God you will not seek forgiveness. *'Fear God and give him glory'*. Why? The angel continues, *'because the hour of his judgment has come. Worship him who made the heavens, the earth, the sea, and the springs of water.'* He made everything that is. Everybody can see these things. Even those who have not heard the gospel have seen the sky, and they should know that it must require a great God to create all that. I have known people who came to a faith in God simply by going out on a starlit night and looking at the sky, gazing at it and thinking about it, and just thinking of their Creator. So the angel is going to see that everybody gets an opportunity. The everlasting gospel will go on being preached even in all these troubles.

Thirdly, he now sees a vision of something which is dismissed in one verse, which we are going to study in detail in chapters 17 and 18 — the fall of Babylon. That name is mentioned right at the beginning of the Bible — the tower of Babel — it is the same name there in Genesis 11. Man's pride in achievement in building up a tower that reaches up to heaven. But Babylon here refers to one worldwide city. I used to think this was the most astonishing prediction of the book of Revelation, that one day everybody will be living in one city. But there are two things that make it believable now to me. First, that such is the drift from country to town that already half of the world's population live in urban areas, the largest being Tokyo with a population of over 35,000,000 (under the latest definition of the metropolitan area there) — and this is expected to rise so that by 2030 it is predicted that 60% of the world's population will reside in urban areas. The second thing is that already towns are interlinked, not only by telephone but by the internet, so that increasingly it would be possible to treat all the cities of the world as the suburbs of one city, and I can well imagine that within the foreseeable future we will be treated as one city council — and the name the Bible gives to that vast metropolis is Babylon, the proud achievement of man.

It is a city that will have a terribly evil influence on the people who come to it — all cities do. Time and again, young people make for the city hoping to find a good time there, and what happens? The city sucks them down into a vortex of evil, loneliness and temptation. You walk through Piccadilly Circus at eleven o'clock at night, any night of the week, and you will see what the city does to youth. This vision is of Babylon falling — not just falling, but fallen — a city that has dragged young people down has vanished, it has gone. Cheer up! These vast urban areas are not going to last forever, they are going to go.

What he sees next is something that is meant to cheer us up, but it is very serious: those who have drunk the wine of

Babylon will drink the wine of God's anger. On those who exploited human weakness, those who built a vast, immoral city for people to come to in which to spend their money, God's anger will be poured out. Those who worshipped the world's dictator and agreed to be tattooed with his mark will also come under God's anger.

I wish the Bible did not have anything about hell, I wish that I could be the kind of preacher who kept off this subject. I wish I could cut these verses out and say, well, they don't fit in with my view of Christ so they can't be Christian, as many do. You will find some of my critics doing just this and saying, 'Well, it doesn't fit in with my idea of Christ, so it can't be God's Word.' I wish I could think that way, but I cannot. Here in this short passage are expressions like this: fire and brimstone, torment, for ever and ever. I cannot get round this, though I wish I could. I wish I could tell you there is no suffering in the next life for others; I wish I could say that there is no hell, that you can forget about it, it was a Victorian way of frightening people to become Christians, but I cannot say it. It is not the ramblings of a medieval priest, it is the revelation of our Lord Jesus, and we must face it.

14:12 makes it clear that the point in mentioning this is that it calls for the endurance of the saints. Since hell is real, do not identify with those who are going there. Since this is what they are working towards, do not climb on the bandwagon, do not get caught, do not get sucked into the stream; endure, even though it is going to be difficult. Keep the commandments of God and the faith of Jesus. That covers your behaviour and your belief — hold on to both.

The next vision, the fifth one, describes the blessedness of those who die in the Lord. The meaning of that phrase *the dead who die in the Lord from now on* is not those who were converted when they were twenty and died when they were seventy, it is those who are still in the Lord when they die. In other words, those who have hung on, those who have not given way to the pressures, those who when they come to die are right with God and in the Lord Jesus — they are blessed people. Why? Because, *'. . . they will rest from their labour, for their deeds will follow them.'* I have heard this text read at funerals — it should not be really, it applies to the last days. It is a special beatitude, one of seven in the book of Revelation, and it is for those in the last days, but we must store it in our hearts in case we need it. To rest from your labours does not mean that heaven is a gigantic lounge. I do not know where people got the vision of a huge patio with deckchairs — this 'rest in peace' idea! You are going to be working in heaven twenty-four hours a day. (They *serve him day and night in his temple*). The word *labour* here does not mean work, it means precisely what it means in a maternity ward: it means pain, it means travail — and blessed are those who are still in the Lord when they die, because they are resting from their pain and their suffering for the sake of the Lord and the gospel.

The words *'their deeds will follow them'* mean that you can take quite a lot with you when you go. You have heard people say 'you can't take it with you when you go' but do not believe it — you cannot take your money with you but you can take an awful lot, you can take a lot of luggage, you can send it on in advance and lay up for yourself treasure in heaven where neither moths nor rust corrupt and thieves do not break through and steal. When you leave this earth and make your journey to glory you can take your deeds for Jesus with you. They will follow you, and what you have done for the Lord will have eternal value and honour. Blessed are those who are still in the Lord when they die, who endure this suffering.

The sixth and seventh visions are both about harvests. This was a favourite metaphor of Jesus about the future: the parable of the wheat and the tares, the parable of the sower, the parable of the seed growing secretly — in all these parables the world's history is like a harvest. The farmer sows the seeds and then they grow, and some other things grow as well — wheat and tares grow along together slowly, surely, and it seems a long time. It seems as if nothing is happening in the field — you do not notice much difference each day — then suddenly the slow process leads to a sudden crisis, and in comes the sickle and in a matter of days it is all gone. Having worked on a farm I understand this picture so clearly. You keep looking at a field and nothing seems to be moving, it does not seem to be heading anywhere. Then you are aware that the heads are forming, then you are aware that they are going a bit yellow, then they go golden, they are ripe and you must go in and reap it. The time has come, and within a day or two it is gone. People say, 'Where is God? What is he doing? It does not seem to be changing, the world seems to be going on.' It is not. There is a harvest coming, there is a process slowly taking place, and one day, suddenly, within a matter of days, it will be gone — 1260 days I am told here, and that is not long in comparison with the history of man. Suddenly it has gone. The harvest has come, the sickle is put in.

The first picture is simply of wheat or corn being harvested, and at the same time we know that tares are burned. Jesus talked about this. Then the picture changes from the corn harvest to the grape harvest, and a vision comes of a great 'winepress of God's wrath'. The grapes are being thrown in, then the feet come and they trample, and the wine which looks so like blood flows.

Steinbeck entitled his novel, one of America's best known, *Grapes of Wrath*, but the book of Revelation is not a novel! Steinbeck wrote fiction, but this is fact. Here we have the grapes of God's wrath and the blood of men — of those who have spurned God. Many reject him; many oppose Jesus Christ. 'We do not want anything to do with God, we want a godless civilisation; we don't want any churches in Babylon, we don't want any Christians here.' God will one day trample under foot those who have said such things.

When we have Holy Communion, the wine in those cups represents blood. Jesus prayed at Gethsemane, *'My Father, if it is possible, may this cup be taken from me.'* Earlier he had said to his disciples, *'Can you drink the cup I am going to drink?'* What is this cup? Throughout the Bible the word 'cup' is used of the wine of God's anger against wickedness, and when Jesus shrank from the cup in Gethsemane he knew that his Father's will was for him to drink his wrath against sin. He did not want to drink it, but finally he said, *'Yet not as I will, but as you will'*, and he drank that cup. When he was put on the cross they offered him another cup of wine, but the night before he had promised his disciples never to drink wine again until he drank it new in the kingdom, so he refused it — but he was drinking a cup of God's wine. We are able to drink that cup because Jesus drank the cup of the wine of God's wrath against sin. That cup becomes for us not a symbol of God's justice, as it was in Bible days, but a symbol of his mercy. It is because he died that we can live, and it is because he faced this that we can join that happy throng and sing a new song around the throne of grace.

GRAPES OF WRATH
Revelation 15 – 16

I shall never forget a time when I read Revelation chapters 15 and 16 in a church. As I got to the word *hailstones* there was a rattle on all the windows and a most incredible hailstorm came — and went two minutes later. When we went out of church the ground was covered with hail, but it was tiny stuff. The congregation looked as if they did not know whether to run or laugh, or what, but it brought home to them in a particularly vivid way the reality of what we were reading.

There are two sorts of difficulty that people have with the book of Revelation. One is the difficulty that comes when they cannot understand what it means. The other is the difficulty that comes when they can understand what it means. When we read these two chapters, apart from a few obscure details, the meaning of it is absolutely clear. I do not need to spend time trying to explain to you what these things mean. You know what boils are, you know what hailstones are, you know what an earthquake is even if you have never been in one. There is nothing that is difficult to understand. The difficulty comes here because we do understand it and because, alas, in our modern days we have such a distorted view of God that when we come to this we instinctively say, 'Well, I can't see that God would do that.' I have lived long enough to discover that it does not really matter whether a person believes in God or not, what really matters is what kind of a God they do or do not believe in. Many people say to me, 'I don't go to church but I don't want you to think that I don't believe in God, because I do.' My next question is, 'What kind of a God do you believe in?' That is the important question — not *whether* you believe in God. The difficulty is that in modern thinking — even in church circles — we have heard so much about *God is love* that we have forgotten that in the same epistle from which we get the text *God is love* a little earlier it says *God is light*. We have heard so many sermons on the mercy of God that we have forgotten his justice. We have heard so often that God pardons sin that we have almost come to think he would never punish it. We have heard so much about *happiness* that we have almost forgotten *holiness*, and forgotten that God's will for us is not primarily that we should be happy but that we should be holy. Therefore the things that we have been looking at in Revelation, to some people, do not fit in with their idea of God. They take the whole truth about God from the prodigal son, or a chapter that is full of mercy, which is much nicer and much more comforting, but that is only half the truth. In Luke 15 you have a picture of God as mercy without any mention of his justice; in Revelation 15 you have a picture of God with justice, and no mention of his mercy —and the truth is both. We must remember this, otherwise we get a distorted view of God.

The book of Revelation presents you with another side to God's character which to human nature may seem not very 'nice', yet is part of the truth. In other words, the subject of this next section is, for better or worse, the *wrath* of God. Immediately there are some who say, 'But surely this is Old Testament stuff.' Let me say two important things. First, there is nothing in the Old Testament more dreadful than the book of Revelation, and this is the New Testament! There is nothing that God does in the pages of the Old Testament that is more horrible than the things he does here. So it is not a case of the New Testament correcting the Old. We cannot evade it that way. Then there are those who say, 'Ah well, this is the book of Revelation, but I believe in the Gospels.' There is nothing said here about God and about Christ that is contradicted anywhere in the four Gospels, and apart from that, this last book in the Bible comes from Jesus, from no-one else — it is the Revelation of Jesus Christ. In other words, you must either accept the God of the book of Revelation or you must reject that God and go away and think up your own kind of god, realising that you have a figment of your own imagination. The God and Father of our Lord Jesus is this God, and you must either take him or leave him, but he is the only God, and he is what he is, and you cannot change that.

Let me go even further because I know what a difficulty this is and many people ask about it. They say, 'Surely, if you want to know what God is like you should look at Jesus. I look at Jesus and I do not see a God like this.' This is a valid question, and I want to answer it this way: Don't you? There is one terrible moment in the life of Jesus when I see in him all that I see in God here; it is a moment when he whipped men out of a holy temple; it is a moment when his eyes blazed with anger; it is a moment when I think even his disciples must have been frightened stiff of him, because he was so angry with the evil that was spoiling his Father's house. I see there the wrath of God. So let us not try and play one part of the Bible off against another, and say the Old Testament God is different from the New Testament, or the book of Revelation is different from the Gospels. I have studied the Bible in depth for more than sixty years, and I have still to find a single contradiction between two statements in this book about God or about Jesus. I have not found one.

We now see the final display of the wrath of God, and then it is over forever. With these chapters the anger of God is spent, and for the rest of eternity it will never again be seen. It is as if God's anger has been building up through the centuries and finally boils over. The Greek language has two words for anger, one is the slow resentment which simmers inside, and the other is the word for boiling over and coming out. You know that there are indeed these two kinds of anger — some people are angry and do not show it, it goes in and it just stays, others boil over and we say they are quick-tempered. The two words are *orge* and *thumos*. *Orge* is a word that means settled-inside anger that does not come out. *Thumos* is a word that means to boil over, to reach the point where you cannot contain your anger and it comes out. It is very interesting that right the way through the New Testament, for the most part the word *orge* is used of the anger of God (there are just one or two exceptions). It is the anger that does not show, as if God is holding it in and containing it. Then, in the book of Revelation, while again there are some exceptions the other way, the word far more frequently used is *thumos* — boiling over. Now the wrath of God shows. People sometimes say, 'Why does God allow war?' 'Why doesn't he do something about wicked men?' Why doesn't he step into this or that conflict, such as Iraq? The answer is that he is not letting his anger show at the moment, he is holding it back. God is angry about Iraq, God is angry about Sudan — I know that because that is the God I read of in these pages. He is very angry about exploitation and cruelty and bloodshed, but he is not showing it at the moment, and that is why people say, 'What's he doing? Where is he?' I just thank God he is not showing it, because as soon as we find out what will happen when he does show it, we do not want it — and you cannot have it both ways. Either we grumble that God does not show his anger and we accept what will happen when he does, or we have to reverse that, but we cannot have it both ways — we cannot say, 'God show your anger, but don't show it'! And here we have the final moment of history, when he shows it very clearly.

Let us set the scene — seven seals, seven trumpets, seven bowls. The seven seals cover the last years of history; the seven trumpets cover the last forty-two months of history. The seven bowls cover the last days of history and will be very brief, and thank God those days are shortened. What will happen? Let us begin with chapter 15, which is a hymn of praise sung in heaven by the martyrs who have overcome the pressures from the world dictator and his right-hand religious leader. Those who have overcome are in glory and they are singing praise. About what? That God is love? No. That God has forgiven their sins? No. That God is merciful? No. What are they praising him for? That he is *just*.

The one thing that makes me feel absolutely sure of the future is that God is fair, just. People often think he is unjust; half the questions I get assume that he is unjust. 'Why does God do . . . when . . . ?' 'Why should God allow an innocent to suffer?' 'Why is God so unjust?' Sometimes I have to say, 'Look, I know God well enough to know that one day you will say to him, "I do not disagree with anything you have done." I know him well enough to know that he will never do anything that is unfair. You do not need to ask all these questions. You do not need to ask what happens to this person if they die without hearing the gospel; what happens about that, and what happens about the other. If you know God well enough you do not ask these questions because you know that whatever he does is fair, just and true.' Have you seen the statue of justice above the Old Bailey in London — the lady with the sword and the scales? Many people think they know something about that statue which is in fact not true at all. I think if you know the statue you will be under the impression that she is blindfolded, on the grounds that she must be blind to be just — but that is not true. Next time you are in London and climb on the roof of the Old Bailey, go up and look at the statue! You will discover that what looks like a bandage from the ground is in fact a headdress round the forehead, and her eyes are wide open. Justice must see, it must not be blind like love. It must see the truth, the whole truth and nothing but the truth. If you are going to have justice you have to have truth, and therefore in courts of law the first thing a witness does is to take a New Testament in his hand and say, 'I swear by Almighty God to tell the truth, the whole truth and nothing but the truth' (or to affirm, instead of making this oath). Here we have a hymn of praise that says, *'You are just in these judgments'*, and the response is heard:

> *'Yes, Lord God Almighty,*
> *true and just are your judgments.'*

The majesty of God comes across here. They are praising God that it is he who will judge the world and no-one else. If these troubles and plagues come upon the world, it is for one reason: the world deserves it — it is just, it is true.

Let me lay out the alternative. Supposing God was not just, supposing you could bribe him, supposing you could get on his good side with extra prayers, supposing you could get round him, supposing the one who was going to judge the human race was not fair and that we could expect injustice in the next world, that would be terrible, would it not? But we need not look forward to that, we can look forward to justice being done.

There is a hymn praising God's majesty and justice, *Thy justice is the gladdest thing creation can behold.* This hymn has six quotations from the Psalms, a quotation from Deuteronomy, a quotation from Isaiah and another from Jeremiah. If you want to be sure you that will know the hymns in heaven then know the Bible on earth, because if you know your Bible down here you will be able to join in very quickly in the songs of heaven — they are made up of biblical sayings and texts.

Not only is this justice praised, it is prepared in the original temple, of which the tabernacle on earth was a copy —right there in the original temple, the eternal temple. We read, *'After this, I looked and in heaven the temple, that is the tabernacle of the Testimony, was opened.'* Here we have the justice of God prepared. No-one could enter the temple until the seven plagues were ended. Why not? Because in the olden days, when a plague came upon the Israelites somebody went into the temple to plead and to pray that it would be stopped. Moses often did this, and the high priest, but when these plagues come no-one can stop them; no-one can pray at that point, 'Lord, please don't.' We can pray now but not then, they must come. And the bowls which are used to pour out these plagues on earth are the very bowls that were used to carry the prayers of the saints. The bowls that carried the intercession up carry the judgement down, and every time you say, 'Your kingdom come' you are praying for this, and the bowl takes your prayer up, and that prayer will one day lead to this. That is chapter 15; you can work out the details for yourself, but it is so straightforward —praising God that he is just. That will come up again later.

In chapter 16 we have seven plagues. Why does God call them bowls instead of trumpets? The simplest answer is a trumpet is a warning, whereas a bowl is not a warning, it is just poured out. In other words, the previous troubles were warnings, these are not, these are judgements. The previous troubles were mercy, to help people to turn to God. These are not mercy, these are justice. Now what are they? Before we look at them in detail may I remind you that there was a time, way back in the Old Testament, recorded in Exodus, when God sent ten plagues on a nation —Egypt. He sent boils, he sent other things, he turned the rivers to blood, and you must have remembered those plagues when reading chapter 16. In other words, God has already done it once, who dares say he will not do it again? God has already done this to the nation of Egypt, and there are no Egyptians today — in fact the people living in Egypt are Arabs from Arabia, they are not Egyptians. Once the mightiest empire the world had ever known, with its pyramids, its sphinxes and its mighty pharaohs — it is all gone. And Egypt's doom was settled the day that Pharaoh refused for the last time to let the Hebrew people go. To stand against God, sooner or later, is to sign your death warrant.

So, God is going to do the plagues again. From this chapter 16 some people have thought — because of some of the plagues — that it refers to nuclear warfare. I do not think that follows; many of these plagues are nothing to do with nuclear bombs. I do not believe the world will end with nuclear conflict. I do not think the Bible tells us that, and therefore I am not worried on that score. I do not think man will end the world by pressing a button —this is God's series of plagues.

First of all, there are boils on the skin, or open running ulcers. And the World Health Organisation will be able to do nothing about it. It almost looks as if it is the actual tattoo of the world dictator on the forehead or the hand which erupts and festers and becomes that, because the people of God are not affected by these, only those who are already marked with a godless dictator. It is poetic justice that people who voluntarily accepted the mark of the beast now receive the mark of God.

Secondly, there is blood in the sea, which is not just red but congealed, which means that all life in the sea dies. I remember going to the Dead Sea and swimming on it. I am sure you have seen pictures. I could sit on it and read a book quite comfortably, and it is quite an unusual experience. There is no life in that sea, which is dead —no fish, nothing in it at all. I can understand why. After you have been in for five minutes you feel like death. It really is a most dreadful place. But one of the most interesting things in the Bible, at the end of Ezekiel, is that God predicts that at the end of history the Dead Sea will be fresh and support life again, and every other sea will go dead and not be able to support life. God can reverse anything; he can make the dead sea live, and the live seas die. That is a terrible plague.

Thirdly, not only the salt water but the fresh water too turns to something like blood and becomes undrinkable, or at least very difficult to drink. Again this is poetic justice. An angel interjects:

> *'You are just in these judgements,*
> *You who are and who were, the Holy One,*
> *because you have so judged;*
> *for they have shed the blood of your saints and prophets,*
> *and you have given them blood to drink*
> *as they deserve.'*

These people have been drinking the blood of martyrs and now they are getting blood to drink from their own taps —how just. God makes the punishment fit the crime.

Fourthly, the atmosphere which protects us from the cosmic rays, the ultra violet rays and the infra red rays of the sun will change, so that the sun is unbearably hot, scorching.

Fifthly, after that, an eclipse of the sun —not like any that we have seen in our lifetimes, but one in which we have gross darkness. This is something Jesus predicted in Matthew's Gospel, which Joel predicted, and it is there all through the Bible. When Jesus died on the cross, as men did their worst to him, God himself gave them a glimpse of what would happen as a result, that it would affect even the sun, which would go out. And for three hours — which is longer than any eclipse — as Jesus died, it was midnight in the middle of the day.

I do not know how you are affected by darkness, but there is in Kentucky a cave called Mammoth Cave, which is reckoned to be the darkest cave in the world. I do not see how that can be, but it is what they say. Tourists are taken into it to experience what real darkness is. The effect on the tourists is interesting. The nervous people talk and talk; they just have to keep talking to make sure that somebody else is there and listening. Others become terribly restless; some scream after only ten minutes. But this is the effect of darkness, it is an unnatural atmosphere for those who have been made in the image of God who is light. Have you ever read Lord Byron's poem *Darkness*, in which finally men set fire to each others' homes just to see each other? It finishes, 'with curses cast them down upon the dust and quash their teeth and howl'. This is the effect of darkness. It is a terrible thing to be living in the dark.

Sixthly, there is a battle. I am sure you have heard that the Jehovah's Witnesses have something to say about Armageddon. There are some points on which they are right, and this is one of them. There is to be a battle at the end of history, and it is to be in the Middle East. I have stood on this spot. Imagine a triangular plain about ten miles across each way, surrounded by hills, and at one key point there is a slight rise; it is a hill called the hill of Megiddo, and from it you can see the whole plain. At its foot is a crossroads, and it is the crossroads of the entire world. The road from Europe down to Arabia comes there; the road from Asia to Africa comes there, and the crossroads is a few hundred yards from the hill of Megiddo. It is the point at which continents meet and there in that plain is to be fought a battle which will signal the last war or battle of history.

It is interesting that Sir Winston Churchill thought that the crucial battle in the last world war would be there, and he sent a party of British army officers to survey Armageddon. He knew his Bible, incidentally, and that influenced him in his thinking. He said, 'I want to know every place to hide, every place to attack, every piece of high ground — I want a survey of that.' As the Italians pressed us back along Egypt, and the Germans came down through Greece, Churchill said, 'It is coming, I can see Armageddon, I can see the British army trapped at Armageddon.' It is fascinating that he thought this way, but he was wrong, because in fact the armies that will converge at that point will not come from the West but from the East. Here we are given a picture of a vast invasion from that part of the world in which 60% of the population lives. There are over 1.3 billion Chinese and over 1.1 billion Indians, and they are all east of the Euphrates. Here in a vision the Euphrates ceases to exist — the barrier goes and the armies march. Why do they come to the Middle East? Because that is where God's purpose has always been worked out; that is where the attention of God's people has been focussed for hundreds of years; that is the future pivot of political history.

Those who have lived to see the Middle East become the focal point of world tension can see all this unfolding. I can see this happening, so clearly, because the nations of the East now want to get through to the West, and they can see the blockage in the middle of the tension in the Middle East. Politically, it is shaping up. If you want to read a book by a politician read Kenneth Kac's *The State of Israel*, and read there how he sees the whole future of world politics focusing around this centre, because here there is an unusual people of God, and here is the pivot and the crossroads.

Finally, the seventh and the last example of God's overflowing anger is literally a bombardment of sinners from below and above: the biggest earthquake from below that has ever been known, that will bring down every major city; and there will be the biggest hailstones from above that have ever been seen. And that is the very end of the anger of God; it is the end of history, the end of civilisation as we have known it; it is the break-up of society. It is the end. Yet for Christians and for all who look to God it will be the beginning. There will come a day when church buildings will be pulled down, and you will see them come down brick by brick; you will see them all become dust. Maybe some will feel unhappy about that — it is understandable at a human level when they carry memories — but the overriding feeling will be that there is something new coming, more exciting, more wonderful than there has ever been before. That is what makes it all so different, and that is why we move on very shortly to the new heaven and the new earth which is to follow, but we have to see that God clears the site first so that he may build a new universe. He has to destroy one so that something new might arise. That is how God deals in re-creation. When he took your life and you were converted, your old life had to go: it had to be crucified, dead, buried in baptism, finished with, then he could build anew. That is how God does his work.

I have two final points before we are through this rather terrible and awe-inspiring chapter 16. First of all, three times in this chapter, men are mentioned as cursing. Secondly, once in this chapter men are mentioned as blessed.

First, three times, in verses 9, 11 and 21, men curse God. Even to the last, that is their reaction to what is just and true. I remember once sitting in a courtroom when a man was sentenced, and it was obviously fair, it was obviously just — and I remember how from the dock he shrieked curses and blasphemies at the judge; it was a horrible moment. I would have respected him as a human being if he had taken his medicine like a man, but he did not. He deserved it and he knew it, yet all he did was curse a man who had been just and true. Such is human nature. One would like to think that to the very last day of history men would say, 'This is the anger of God, we must get right with God', yet they do not. And the fact that they curse God is virtually saying, 'God, we are innocent and you are unjust; you are in the wrong, not us.' That is a terrible thing to say to a God who is just and true, and yet that is what they do. Three times in these two chapters God is said to be *just* (15:3, 16:5, 16:7). The angels and the martyrs say that God is just and true. And three times men curse him for it. Even Job, that saintly man of God, did not do this. He got boils on the skin, he went through trouble, and his wife said, *'Curse God and die!'* — and he would not do so. *In all this, Job did not sin in what he said.* He never cursed God.

Have you ever gone into a factory, or worked on a farm, and listened to the language? I used to milk cows on a farm at four in the morning every day, and the man milking cows opposite had the dubious reputation of being able to swear the longest without repeating himself; there were fourteen workers and that was his 'distinction'. Out of all his swearing, at least a third of the words he used were blaspheming against God. The things I had to listen to at that time gave me a little insight into the kind of language there will be on earth when God shows that he is angry with men.

But there is one verse that has blessing in it—16:15. The words of Jesus, at the very lowest ebb of human history, at the very worst moment, are these: *'Behold, I come like a thief! Blessed is he who stays awake . . . .'* When it is dark, burglars are on the prowl; they come to rob men, to take something away from them and Jesus is saying, *'I come like a thief!'* (See also Matthew 24:43, 2 Peter 3:10 and 1 Thessalonians 5:2.) What does it mean? He comes to take things from men; he has come to take the kingdom and the power and the glory from men and give them back to God — he comes like a robber. Blessed are those who are watching for him because he will not take anything from them; they will not lose anything when he comes. *'Blessed is he who stays awake and keeps his clothes with him, so that he may not go naked and be shamefully exposed.'* A Roman sentry who was posted on duty and who fell asleep was stripped naked and exposed to the ridicule of his fellow soldiers—that was the punishment. Christians need to remain awake, clothed and ready.

When the night is blackest, it is just before the dawn; when things are worst, it is just before the best; when men's hopes and cities are crashing, it is just before Jesus comes, and therefore Christians are to watch and be ready so that we do not lose anything, so that we are not left naked without the things that we cherish. Keep alert, keep awake, watching for these events. Those who are watching and awake are blessed.

METROPOLITAN PROSTITUTE
Revelation 17–18

Before looking at this section, I suggest reading Genesis 11:1–9, the story of Babel, which eventually became Babylon. That was the beginning, but they did not leave it there and, although people stopped building it at that stage, they came back later, and I now want to go to Daniel 4:29ff. When it reached its heyday the greatest city in the then known world and the famous Hanging Gardens of Babylon were one of the seven wonders of the world under king Nebuchadnezzar. Then read Isaiah 13:17ff which is about a vision Isaiah the prophet had concerning Babylon. Finally, move on to Jeremiah and read Jeremiah 51 and the last words said on Babylon in the Old Testament, from verse 41.

You may have seen photographs or pictures in books of Babylon today. There is nothing there but a heap of dust and rubble, except jackals and wild beasts and birds. And because the Arabs believe that demons dwell in the city ruins they will not stay overnight within them, so every night even an archaeologist has to leave the city and go back to the camp outside. That is what happened to the Babylon of the Old Testament. Now we are going to look at a chapter that is all about Babylon in the New Testament (Revelation 17). Having read the history in brief of the old Babylon, you will understand this part much better.

The best commentary on the book of Revelation is your daily newspaper. I do not know whether you have discovered just how relevant this book is to what is happening in the world.

For example, there have long been movements which seek to unite the world religions. We have read of many over the past few decades, groups which seek to incorporate beliefs. In the European Union there were calls for there to be mention of God in the constitution, to reflect the Judaeo-Christian heritage of the continent, but these calls were opposed and the idea was scrapped. There is a prevailing desire not to offend other religions and groups. If we do not want to listen to these things we can bury our heads in the sand like ostriches, but these are things that are going on, and as we read our daily papers we see the truth of Revelation ever more clearly. When I began my ministry almost sixty years ago there were things in the book of Revelation that seemed to me incredible; many of those things today seem so ordinary and so real that I wonder why I ever doubted.

Our subject now is Babylon, and that stands for the fact that when we have one world government and one world religion there will have to be a political and religious headquarters. There will have to be a centre of government for the world dictator, and Babylon is the name given to the greatest city of the future from which world government and world religion will radiate to every corner of the earth. These two chapters above describe the downfall of that great city, in one hour. It is a very difficult section of the book of Revelation in the sense that there is a lot of strange wording in it — with sentences such as, '. . . *he once was, now is not and yet will come'*. Again, I plead with you not to get bogged down in the details, get the main picture and then you will begin to understand the details.

It begins with John being shown a vision — a terrible portrait which I would imagine very few art galleries would even consent to hang. It is a picture of a woman who is very clearly a woman of loose morals. She is described as a harlot, she is gorgeously apparelled, she is obviously drunk, she has a filthy cup filled with something, and she is sitting on an ugly animal. Can you imagine any worse picture? No wonder John marvelled at the brazen wantonness of the picture — that it should be revealed by God (*'When I saw her I was greatly astonished.'*) And yet it is a horrible picture for a horrible thing. We must face the fact that world population is not only exploding rapidly — almost doubling since 1970, with 6.6 billion people in the world and expected to rise to 9 billion by 2050 — but there is a terrific move into the towns and cities. People do not want to live in the country, in the wilderness, any more, they want the bright lights, the facilities, so the young generation makes for the town as soon as it can, and from the town makes for the city, and wants a flat in the city if possible —this is the drift. Coupled with the fact that almost half the world's population is under the age of twenty-five, we can see the beginnings of an absolute nightmare.

Almost forty years ago I read an imaginary fictional work of city life set in about 1995, in which you dare not leave your house after dark, there are too many violent youngsters outside your own door. That was not panicking, that was not an imaginary fancy, because in parts of many cities of America this has long been so, with people having to have guard dogs around their own houses because of the violence in the streets and the fear stalking through the shadows. We can see the same violence in a few of our cities in Britain, with violent gangs which shoot innocent children dead. This then is the drift, and the Bible does not see any reversal of this drift, it sees things heading up until finally there is one vast city in touch with all other cities and towns and which becomes the apex of all the worst that a city can be.

Another book which I once read, and which influenced many people's thinking, was *The Secular City*, by Harvey Cox. I am almost ashamed to confess that he is a Baptist. But after giving a brilliant diagnosis of the problems of city life and urbanisation, and the fact that in the cities religion tends to disappear, he then goes on to say he can see God in all this, and that he feels this is a divine move. I just want to get hold of Harvey Cox sometimes and say, 'Do you know the book of Revelation? Can you not see that this secularisation of life is not of God?' This depersonalisation of life, so that people living in vast cities do not even know their next door neighbour, they do not know who lives in the flat below and the flat above, they are in rabbit hutches of flats, and they are just there, home to watch television and back to work to get a bit more money to buy a flat screen set. God never ordained this kind of life. And it is there in the cities that vice and perversion breed, and where people in the anonymity of a large community can do despicable things. This is not a divine move, it is a satanic move. And according to these chapters there will come a point where the people of God will have to get out of the cities. Thank God for the Christian people who are in them at the moment; thank God for city missions, but there will come a day when God will tell his people to come out of the cities. He brought his people out of the Babylon of the Old Testament; and, as we know, he says in the New Testament, *'Come out of her, my people . . . .'*

Here then is a picture of the woman sitting on the animal. John is perplexed; it is a mystery to him. Who is she? What is she doing? He recognises the animal as the beast, already seen in an earlier chapter, whom we now know represents that world dictator. And there she is sitting on the beast — they belong together. We learn who she is in the chapter. The woman is Babylon. We know all that this word signifies. To the ancient Jew 'Babylon' meant a cesspool of greed, cruelty, godlessness and lust. It became a byword among the nations for all that is rotten in urban development, and Babylon here stands for the same thing. It is not, I think, the same city, but it stands for a vast metropolis controlling the world. Its size is the largest ever, it is called the great city, its power is that it influences all continents, its wealth is clearly there in gold, jewels and other things. Its luxury is mentioned; its vice is mentioned; its superstition is mentioned. It has misled the nations by its sorcery — which includes such things as magic and spiritism. And above all, there is its cruelty — she is *drunk* with *blood.* Whose blood? ... *the woman was drunk with the blood of the saints, the blood of those who bore testimony to Jesus* — 'the saints' in a dirty city lived straight and clean. In a dishonest city they live in an honest manner; they are people in a godless city who praised God and bore testimony to Jesus. She did not like people like that around, and she killed them one by one.

This, then, is the mystery of the city. I do not think it will be, as some Christians believe, a rebuilt Babylon on the river Euphrates. The reason why I do not believe that is that Isaiah said it *will never be rebuilt,* and it never has been. Nor do I think, as I am afraid some commentators have made it, that the scarlet woman is Rome, either politically or religiously. I know there are seven hills in Rome, but I think that is a coincidence — the seven hills referred to here are a city at the end of history, not a city way back in those days. It is a clue that will help us to recognise it, but I think that is coincidental that it is Rome. Whether it will be an already existing city blown up in size — London, Tokyo, Moscow, Paris, New York — I do not know. It may be a completely new city. It will be within sight of the sea, but then most big cities are, so that does not help us either. All I can say is that you will know when it comes. When you see one vast city on seven hills, within sight of the ocean, controlling the world, that is Babylon and you will be in no doubt — you will not need me to tell you what it is.

Her influence is described as that of *the great prostitute*. Now many have thought that that refers to a lax sexual life in the city. There are indications that such an interpretation is valid, to a degree. Certainly that would seem to be true of the city here. This city, in relation to the world, has behaved exactly as a prostitute behaves. I saw them walking the streets of Paris in a way that they do not walk the streets of London now. What is their attitude to people? It was quite obvious — as long as they got the money they would offer any pleasure, regardless of moral principles. That is the heart of it: regardless of any morality, I will give you anything you want if you will give me money. Here we have a picture of a city that is money mad, that will do anything to get money, that will do it to bring the crowds to the city, and in exchange for pleasure get more and more wealth. No wonder the traders come, no wonder the kings come, no wonder that this is the commercial centre of world civilisation. There is money here, there is pleasure here, so that businessmen can combine both. I am astonished how often today I have heard from different places how many firms instruct their chief salesmen to lay on girls, as well as hotels, for visiting businessmen from overseas. This is happening in Britain today, whether you like it or not — business and pleasure, money and sex all wrapped up together in one big bundle in a vast city.

But this is not really so incredible, is it? It is part of life, it is a development of what we already know in our country, just multiply it. Here she is with a cynical policy of expediency, with an abandonment to impulses and the desires of the moment, ready to sacrifice anything sacred for gain and with a contempt for goodness and purity. For one of the most devastating results of harlotry is on the character rather than the body, and the result in the character is a cynicism and a break-up of all standards and a despair of people, and that is what is happening here.

That is the woman, but what about the beast? We have already seen the beast in chapter 13. Here certain details are explained: *'he once was, now is not, and yet will come.'* Cutting through all the many interpretations, it looks to me as if he will be a lesser ruler, and will then disappear from the scene, either by living quietly or even by dying, and will then — supernaturally, by devilish power — come back to rule. And when you see a ruler who gets a certain power then goes right out of the picture and then comes back with universal power, that is the kind of picture I get. He is a man who will control other kings and kingdoms, for the seven heads refer to seven kings. Later he is said to have ten horns and the meaning is given to us: ten satellite governors, all of whom acknowledge his rule. Again, we cannot press the details because we have not arrived at this point in history, we can only say that when we see a ruler with ten satellite governors under him controlling the world we will know that the day has come. And this beast and his kings attack the Lamb of God. They set their faces against Christ, and therefore against Christians, but the Lamb will defeat them because he is King of kings and he is Lord of lords.

There is only one man who can be called King of kings and Lord of lords — it is Jesus, the Son of God. The beast is the Antichrist and will challenge Christ. But here is the most remarkable twist at the end of chapter 17. God, in his most amazing control of men, will cause the beast and the kings themselves to destroy their own capital city, to turn against the prostitute. I do not know how that will come about. I do not know what made Nero cause Rome to be burned to the ground, if that is what he did, but I know that God is able to cause men to destroy themselves; he does not need to do anything but take the brakes off their twisted minds, and through some twisted thinking they will come to see the city as their enemy and will destroy it —and Babylon will be destroyed, not so much by God as by the rulers of the world themselves.

So in chapter 18 we hear the reaction to the fall of Babylon among the people who knew her. We hear of her fate, which is a just fate. She was drunk with the blood of martyrs, she must now drink the wine of her impure passion. And it is at this point that God warns his own people to *come out of her.* And I say again, there will come a day when every Christian will have to get out of that vast, wicked city. They will try to persuade others to leave with them I am quite sure, though I question whether they will succeed any more than Noah, who took only seven others to safety. The description of all her punishment and her plagues I leave you to read; it is straightforward and you do not need me to explain it. It is just stated that she becomes like Sodom and Gomorrah. The only trace that men have been able to find of Sodom and Gomorrah is one cemetery.

Now look at her followers: the kings, the merchants, the sailors. The kings look at this city and are *Terrified at her torment*; the merchants of the earth *will weep and mourn over her because no-one buys their cargoes any more*; and they and the seafarers are saying *'Woe! Woe, O great city . . . .'*

This is one of the most poetic sections in the book of Revelation. In verse after verse we read of the permanent devastation of the city. There will be no more music, no more trade; never again.

Look ahead for a moment to chapter 19. You have probably heard Handel's *Messiah* and thrilled to that lovely music. Perhaps you have found your heart lifted up to heaven as you have listened to the *Hallelujah Chorus*. Did you know that it is praising the Lord for the end of Babylon? Did you know that the word *hallelujah* means 'praise the Lord'? Now how do you like Handel's *Messiah*? Now what do you think about the hallelujah chorus? You see, this is a great test as to whether you see things from man's or God's point of view. If you see things primarily from fallen man's point of view you cannot shout *hallelujah* when you hear of these things. But if you see things from God's point of view, and see God looking down on cities in which young people are being brought up in godless environments, and see the vice which they are learning about from their earliest years, and see the cruelty and the loneliness and the people driven to desperate measures, then when God ends this city you will shout, 'Hallelujah, the Lord God omnipotent reigns.' So in chapter 19 we have the *roar of a great multitude in heaven*, who are shouting:

'Hallelujah!
Salvation and glory and power belong to our God, for true and just are his judgments.

He has condemned the great prostitute,
who corrupted the earth by her adulteries.
He has avenged on her the blood of his servants.' And again
they shouted:
'Hallelujah!'
The smoke from her goes up for ever and ever.

That is the origin of the *Hallelujah Chorus*. It is an expression of thanks to God that the city has come to an end, and that all the vice, the dirt and the crime, and all the sin that lurked in its streets, can no more corrupt the earth. The great cities that have been built, and are currently building up before our very eyes today, must be a heartbreak to God with all that goes on in them, and therefore as Christians we look further than this.

The book of Revelation is all the time clearing the site. God has set within us the desire to take down the old and to build the new. When God clears Babylon out of the way, why does he do it? The answer is so simple: that there may come a city whose builder and maker is God, a new Jerusalem adorned as a bride for her husband coming down out of heaven, a city with clean streets of gold, a city with no shadows where evil lurks, a city full of light and beauty. He has to get rid of the city of men before the city of God can come. That is the story of Revelation 17 and 18. We are getting so near the new heaven and the new earth.

THE BRIDE WORE WHITE
Revelation 19

Jesus was always surprising people. As a boy of twelve he surprised his mother and his foster father with his religious maturity. As a man he was constantly doing unexpected things. For example, his disciples were surprised that he had time for children. Then again on Palm Sunday he surprised them all by weeping, and by riding on an ass, and by going into the temple to turn out the money changers instead of into the fortress to get rid of the Romans. Later he surprised the disciples by submitting to crucifixion and not doing anything about it. I suppose the biggest surprise was when he rose from the dead —they just did not expect that either. Then he surprised them again by ascending to heaven. They thought they had him back with them and then he left them. He was full of surprises, always doing things that people did not expect him to do or to be. And the reason is that he was a far deeper and more complex character than any of them had realised. This applies at the human level. Sometimes I have heard a person say of someone else, 'I never thought they had that in them, they really surprised us.' Or sometimes they say, 'What a revelation that was, I never knew they could be like that.' This is the character of Jesus, and just when you think you know him and have got him all summed up and nicely pictured in your mind, there he goes and does something so unexpected that you see him in a completely new light, and you say, 'I never knew Jesus was like that at all.' And you might even say, 'What a revelation.' This book is the Revelation of Jesus, and it reveals a picture of Jesus that some people never dream exists. They have got him nicely fitted into their minds, and they think they know exactly what Jesus is like, and then suddenly they read the book of Revelation and they think, 'Well, I never thought he was like that at all; I never knew he had that in him.' The book of Revelation shows us Jesus in all the complexity of his character, doing things that nobody dreams that he would do, and showing his character in quite a new light.

Let us look at some of the surprises. Here we have a much bigger view of Christ. I have three names: John David Pawson. 'John' is after one grandfather, 'David' after another, and 'Pawson' after all my forefathers, but three is ample for me. Some people have just two, and that I think is quite enough. The Queen, I think, has nine or ten, or even more, so the more important a person, the more names they have. But names indicate different character when they are added to a person bit by bit, and at school we added names to describe the character or appearance of our peers. Do you know how many names Jesus has in the Bible? It is not twenty, it is not fifty, it is not one hundred, it is not two hundred, it is two hundred and fifty! In this chapter we are told that he has a name here which no-one knows yet, so we are going to learn even more names for Jesus in heaven when we see his whole character revealed. But here he is presented to us as the bridegroom, as the judge and as the conqueror, and while there are glimpses of these titles earlier in the Bible, we see them fully here.

At first sight the rejoicing multitude at the beginning of chapter 19 is exactly what people expect. There is no surprise to look into heaven and find a whole lot of people singing the 'hallelujah chorus'. The surprise is what they sing *hallelujah* about. The word is Hebrew for 'praise the Lord' — but it is the only word that Christians all over the world use in exactly the same pronunciation. You could go to any nationality, any language and shout *hallelujah*, and all the Christians would turn around. Not even the name of Jesus is the same in all the different languages, but hallelujah is, it is a universal word. But it is never used in the New Testament except in Revelation 19. It is used frequently in the Psalms, from Psalm 100 to Psalm 150. And you will find that in the Psalms and in Revelation chapter 19 it is used for the same thing—the destruction of wicked people (see, for example, Psalm 104:35). The surprise here is a bunch of people singing 'hallelujah' because the largest city in the world has been utterly destroyed. Some people think: how heartless, how cruel — don't they have any feelings? Why sing hallelujah about a thing like that?

There are two reasons why we find this hard. One is simple: we have not yet seen Babylon in all its foul, evil power. We have seen something of the evil of cities but we have not seen anything like Revelation 18 yet. When we do, we shall really want to shout 'hallelujah' when it is over. We hear some pretty horrible things about cities in America and Britain where you do not dare to leave your hotel after dark and walk the streets; cities where you carry an envelope in your pocket with money in it, to give to somebody who holds you up because it is cheaper than your life, and if you do not have money you are likely to be shot; drug addicts need money so badly they will do anything to get it. We have seen and heard something of city life. Imagine that on the scale of which we read in chapter 18, and you will sing the hallelujah chorus when that is ended.

The second reason why we do not feel like saying 'hallelujah' when we hear of the destruction of a large city is this: that we are not holy enough to feel happy when that happens. Our sympathies are with the city. We like the sophisticated city life, we take part in it, we enjoy it and therefore we are not sufficiently detached from it to shout 'hallelujah' when it goes. For these two reasons — that we have not seen city life at its worst yet and that we do not see things from God's point of view as we should, but from man's — we do not get so excited about the possibility of the ending of the great capital city of the world. The 'multitude in heaven' are seeing things from God's point of view, and they are singing *hallelujah* because the evil city has fallen. That is the negative reason — God's retribution has come upon the evil city.

The positive reason is this: now God can begin to show what he can do when he reigns. The end of man's power is the beginning of God's. The end of the reign of the human dictator is the beginning of the reign of God — *'Hallelujah! For our Lord God Almighty reigns.'* Would you not love to see God reigning on the throne of this world? He does not at the moment; he reigns on the throne of heaven but not on the throne of earth. The devil is the 'prince of this world' and 'the god of this world', and the whole world lies in the power of the evil one — that is why it is in the mess it is. Therefore, when we see the world's dictatorships come to an end, and God's kingdom begin, we will shout 'hallelujah'. Of course we will, we will be thrilled to bits!

What is the first thing that will happen when God reigns? The answer is: a marriage. A school teacher came to me a long time ago and said, 'I have been asked a question by some of my pupils and I can't answer it. The question is, why was Jesus never married?' I said, 'There is a very simple answer to that: he is going to be.' Then she looked at me as if I was a bit strange, and said, 'What do you mean?' I said, 'Jesus is the bridegroom, he is going to get married. You can read all about his wedding at the end of the Bible.' It is the most thrilling wedding service that there ever will be, and here it is described. It follows immediately from the ending of the great prostitute, the city of Babylon. When the prostitute is out of the way, the bride can come. When all the wrong relationships are ended, the right relationships can begin — and we move straight from the harlotry of chapter 18 to the bride of chapters 19, 20 and 21, and we now move into the marriage supper of the Lamb. So let us get it quite clear that Jesus is going to get married. To whom? The answer: to his bride. But who is that? Who will have the holy privilege of being the bride of Christ? For female readers, what would you think if Jesus wanted to marry you? I put it like that not because I want to be crude or irreverent but because I want to make it real. The bride includes every Christian who goes to church. The church's attitude to Christ is to be the attitude of the bride looking forward to being wholly her husband's.

There are two things that need to be made ready: the garments and the guests. The first thing is the garment — that white robe. Walk round the high streets and see the girls looking longingly and imagining themselves in this or that. But the church's attitude ought to be just as excited, and thinking: now what am I going to wear? We are told here that the first concern of the bride is to be clothed in fine white linen. That is still the same custom we observe today, to be married in white, pure and clean. And the fine linen is the righteous deeds of the saints. You cannot buy this wedding gown, you can only live this wedding gown, and how you live is going to be what you wear in that day.

The second thing of course are the guests. At this point the picture, the metaphor, breaks down. You cannot press it too far

213

because the guests are the bride and the bride are the guests. In fact there will be nobody there but the bride and nobody there but the guests, and one thing is absolutely clear: nobody will be there except by invitation. You cannot gatecrash this wedding, but when the invitation goes out you can refuse it, and there will be people who will not share in it because they refuse to come. Christ told many stories about weddings like this, and he said the invitations went out and this person said 'no' and this other person refused too, but those who have come, those who have responded to the call of Jesus, will be there — they have had an invitation. Blessed are those who are invited; it is the best thing that ever happened to you to receive the invitation of Christ to come and join him in heaven. 'From heaven he came and sought her to be his holy bride.' And everyone who believes in Jesus is going to be married one day to the best person of all, forever — not even till death us do part.

John is so thrilled with all this, so busy writing it down, that he makes a mistake that people have made ever since: he confuses the message with the messenger. Because he gets a wonderful message through this angel, he starts worshipping the messenger. Never do that. Whatever message you hear from a pulpit or from anyone else, however wonderful it is, never confuse the message with the messenger. If I did not have this book I could give my congregation nothing worthwhile. And in so far as I give them what this book says, they get a wonderful message. If I just give them my opinions then what is the point? In so far as I did that I would be abusing the pulpit. My job is not to be skilful in oratory; it is not to tickle people's fancy or amuse or entertain with new notions and ideas, my job is simply to tell the truth — but what a wonderful privilege. I am like this angel and like the brethren mentioned here — just their fellow servant, that is all. We have different callings in the church's task, but we are just fellow servants. Never use the phrase 'Mr so and so's church' — that is the kind of confusion that John fell into here, and he thought what a marvellous message, it must be a wonderful messenger, and he fell down before the angel — and the angel said, *'Do not do it! I am a fellow-servant with you and with your brothers who hold to the testimony of Jesus. Worship God!' For the testimony of Jesus is the spirit of prophecy.'* There is a mention of the Trinity: the spirit of prophecy, the testimony of Jesus, the worship of God, and these three are related. When somebody brings a wonderful message it is because the Spirit of prophecy has given to that person the testimony of Jesus, in order that people might worship God.

The third thing we notice in this chapter is the greatest surprise of all. Here comes the bridegroom, but what a sight! Here is a Jesus that people have never seen before. This complex character of Jesus is seen in a completely new light. One thing is absolutely clear: though Jesus was not a fighter when he visited the earth the first time, he will be when he comes the second time. In other words, you cannot limit Christ, or even confine him to a pacifist category. Here is a man who makes war; 'the Son of God goes forth to war'. When he visited earth the first time he quite deliberately chose an ass on which to ride because he came in peace. But when he visits earth the second time he comes not on an ass but on a horse, which is always the warrior's mount. He is coming to fight. You see, the difference between his two comings is this: the first time he comes to save and to heal; the second time he comes to judge and to kill. And if you cannot fit both of these into a whole picture of Jesus then you do not know him well enough yet, you have only seen part of his character, you have too simple and too small a view of our Lord. Now it stretches us and there are many who feel so uncomfortable with this view of Jesus that they say, 'Well, I am going to run away from this book back to the Gospels.' But you cannot do that, you are running away from Jesus if you do.

Look first at this picture. Look first at this horse. It is a horse of war, a charger, no longer a donkey. A donkey is no use in fighting, but a horse is. And he has cavalry with him. Look at his titles: he is *Faithful and True*, keeps his promise, keeps his word. Look at his intention. He comes to judge and to make war in righteousness. Those who ridicule the idea of a just war are face to face with this statement. Here will be the first — perhaps the only — just war in history; it will be a war that is just and righteous. Look at his appearance, his flaming eyes. Nothing is hidden from these eyes; there is blazing anger in them. And there are many crowns upon his head — boundless sovereignty. Look at his names. There is one name that we know — the Word of God; there is another name we do not know, because here is a new facet of his personality showing which requires a new name. Look at his clothes — they are a mixture of white and red; they are a robe of linen, with blood. Sometimes when I take the communion, and look at the white bread and the red blood, I think of Jesus who is coming again. There are the same colours — the white linen and the red blood, the mixture.

Look at his army behind him. Jesus said in his lifetime on earth, *'Do you think I cannot call on my Father, and he will at once put at my disposal more than twelve legions of angels?'* That means twelve thousand troops. And here he is going to use them, against men. The fact that he did not use them on his first visit does not mean that he never will. Look at his weapons — the sword, the rod. The sword proceeds from his mouth. Christ fought with words, and his words can kill as well as heal. Above all, look at his title: King of kings and Lord of lords. What a title! No matter how many kings there have been, there is one king supreme. I remember watching the coronation service of Queen Elizabeth II. She was handed the Bible at one point and she was told that this was the only law to which she was subject: Here is the royal law, these are the lively oracles of God. In other words, you may be Queen over everybody else in England, your word may be law over England, but you are under someone else's Word and someone else's law. Nobody is higher than Jesus; he is 'King of kings' and 'Lord of lords'. What a picture of Jesus!

The interesting thing is this. This picture is exactly what the Jews hoped was happening on Palm Sunday. They got it all wrong. The only thing they got wrong, of course, was the timing. Many people think that what they got wrong was that they misunderstood Jesus — they did not. They knew their Bibles well and they knew that God had promised to send a conqueror to relieve them from their enemies. They knew that God promised to set Jerusalem free. The only thing they got wrong was the timing, and when Jesus came riding in on the ass that day they did not realise that he was not coming yet to restore the kingdom to Israel. So they said '*hosanna*' which means save us now. '*Blessed is he who comes in the name of the Lord!*' That comes from a passage where God promises to fight their enemies and defeat them — so they were right to cry that, but they had the wrong time. Jesus cannot come to defeat the enemies until he has first come to die for them, and that was what they had got wrong.

217

When Jesus left the earth, at the ascension, they said to him, *'Lord, are you at this time going to restore the kingdom to Israel?'* They wanted to know when he was going to fulfil that promise. He did not say, 'Well, I am sorry, I am never going to, you have it all wrong', he said: *'It is not for you to know the times or dates the Father has set by his own authority.'* He would come and do it, but not yet.

This is perhaps where so many people have misunderstood Jesus. They thought he chose an ass because he never would fight, but that is not true, it was because it was not yet God's time to restore the kingdom. But here he is coming to do what they hoped he would do on Palm Sunday and had not done.

So in the rest of the chapter we have a passage which I find almost too disturbing to read. It is another invitation to a supper, but it is not to people to come and eat the flesh of birds, it is to birds to come and eat the flesh of people. One of the most awful sights after a battle in the Middle East is the sky. It is bad enough on the ground, but the sky is filled with vultures and buzzards that seem to smell blood fifty miles away. They circle and pounce, and sit there waiting for the battle to be over, knowing they will have a feed. Here we have an extraordinary passage in which an angel says to the birds, *'Come, gather together for the great supper of God, so that you may eat the flesh of kings, generals, and mighty men, of horses and their riders, and the flesh of all people, free and slave, small and great.'* Why do so many lie on the battlefield? Because they thought they could fight Jesus and get away with it. Anybody who thinks they can defy the King of kings and Lord of lords and win is an utter fool. And all these, led by that world dictator and by that archbishop of paganism the false prophet, gather to defy Christ when they hear he is coming to

218

fight; they lose the battle together, and it is all over for them.

The beast and the false prophet are removed from earth forever. They do not die, they are thrown alive into something worse; the kings die, the generals die, and Jesus has won the last world war. That is a different Jesus, is it not? But this is the Jesus who is coming. It is the Jesus who came on Palm Sunday, and it is the Jesus who will come again. *'Hallelujah! For our Lord God Almighty reigns.'* He will have the victory.

DEVIL'S DUNGEON
Revelation 20

We turn to some remarkable revelations of the future in chapter 20. What is God doing? He is getting rid of all evil, step by step. He has destroyed the city, he has got rid of the beast, the dictator; he has removed the false prophet, and now he is going to deal with the devil. He does so not in one swoop but in three stages. He restrains him for a period and stops him having any influence on earth, he releases him for a very little while, and then he consigns him to the lake of fire, and the devil will never trouble anyone again.

Now let us look at these stages. The first thing we have to face is this period of one thousand years, often referred to as the millennium, which is the Roman word for a thousand years. I think it is very sad that Christians have argued so much and disagreed so much about the millennium, almost unchurched each other over it, and I am certainly not going to do that. There are, broadly speaking, three views which I want to mention quite briefly. All I will do is mention them, then let you know which one of the three I am going to build on.

There is the *amillennial* view which says this is not a period of time at all — it refers to something else, quite what we are not sure, but it is only mentioned here in scripture, say these people, and therefore it is not terribly important. It is too material a concept to believe, therefore it is better to believe that Christ will come again, finish everything evil, and take us all straight to heaven. My problem with this is that it is mentioned six times. How many times does God have to say a thing before we take it seriously? Furthermore, there are many promises of God in the Bible that are not fulfilled anywhere in history, and there must surely be some opportunity for God to keep his word towards the end of history.

The second view is called the *post-millennial* which claims that the millennium will be established not by Christ coming but by the church as missionary work, and that the church is called to establish the reign of Christ, and that one day the church will succeed and the whole world will come into the church, and the gospel will be believed by all the nations, and that then we shall have the millennium, at the end of which Christ will come. Once again, when Christ comes he will straightaway take us to glory with him. But what about the devil? And what about the increasing population —most of whom do not become Christians? And what about the rest of the book of Revelation, which does not seem to envisage a growth of the kingdom and an increasing mastery over evil?

The third view is the only one which seems to do justice to the Bible and fit naturally and easily into this passage. That is the view that when Jesus comes again — having got rid of all the evil and conquered it— he will then reign on earth for a period, before he takes us to glory. And that he will demonstrate what the earth can be like when he is on the throne. Now this is the clear implication and meaning of this passage: he will come again, clear the evil out of the road, and then he will reign, for this period specified. In other words, he comes not only negatively to get rid of evil, but positively, to bring good. Now think of what the world would be like if Jesus ran it. You realise that democracy is not the divine order of government, autocracy is what God meant, provided you have got the right autocrat. And you cannot find any man who is pure enough to do this, until Jesus comes again. For the first time the prayer that you pray every Sunday will be answered — 'Your kingdom come . . . on earth as it is in heaven.' You pray for that, how do you think it will come? When the King comes, the kingdom will come, and not until.

Think what will happen when Jesus reigns here. First we will have world peace. There will be no more armies, navies or air forces — I have the Word of God's authority for that. (*They will beat their swords into plowshares and their spears into pruning hooks.*) There will not only be peace among men, there will even be peace among the animals. (See Isaiah 11:6–7.) Think of that: peace right through the whole earth, even animals not preying on one another. These are promises of God —when will they be fulfilled on earth if there is not going to be a reign of Christ on earth? The world will be filled with justice for the oppressed, for the poor, and since we will not be spending gigantic sums on things that God does not want us to do, I believe everybody will get enough to eat. It cost 300 billion dollars (more in today's money) to put one man on the moon. When Jesus reigns we will not throw away money on things like that, I honestly believe it, because in any case, later we will be able to travel anywhere in the universe with him without rockets! So I foresee a reign of peace, prosperity and justice when the earth will be filled with the knowledge of God, as the waters cover the sea. I do not think the church will do that; Christ will be needed to do that at his coming.

John sees a group of people reigning with Jesus. And as John looks, he sees a whole lot of people who have been dead and are alive again. This is referred to as the first resurrection, and it clearly refers to those who believe in Jesus. As he looks at that company reigning over the earth, the meek having inherited the earth at last, he sees a special group among them.

He saw the martyrs reigning over the world. People who had been beheaded for Jesus, and had not worshipped the beast or his image and had not received the mark are reigning over the nations; it is a remarkable reversal and they reign with Christ.

Here is an important biblical truth. There are two deaths and two resurrections. The first death is physical and it separates you from men and from this world; the second death is worse and it separates you from God and from the next world. And those who take part in the first resurrection will not know the second death — you may well know the first but you will not know the second. Therefore, there is a period between the two resurrections. The Christians will rise long before the other dead will see the daylight again. This is what 1 Corinthians 15 says: *Christ, the firstfruits; then, when he comes, those who belong to him.* Did you notice the two 'then's? There is a gap. Resurrection takes place in three stages: *Christ, the firstfruits;* [that has already passed] *then, when he comes, those who belong to him* [that is the next resurrection.] *Then the end will come . . .* [And we will move on to the final resurrection a little later.] Here is very important biblical truth: *Blessed and holy are those who have part in the first resurrection.* You will be alive before everybody else; you will join the martyrs and you will reign with Christ. Are you ready to reign? You are part of the royal family, you are going to reign over the earth one day with Christ.

At the end of this period, Satan is released. Why? To prove the communists wrong. Before you wonder where on earth I am going now, let me explain. The communists believe, quite firmly, that provided you have a period of perfect government, human nature will change. They were convinced of this, and that was why they worked for world government — they honestly believed that if you can have perfect government, human nature is redeemed from sin and you will never have any more trouble with sin. How foolish to believe that! After one thousand years of perfect government, God demonstrates that even if Christ ran the earth people will not change, and he releases Satan, and Satan manages to persuade a whole lot of men and women to follow him again. It is his last despairing fling, and God deals with it like that, and Satan is finished. I think God does this to show that those who think that perfect government is the answer are wrong. Even if Jesus were running the government in this country, there would still be people who would choose Satan rather than Jesus. The only reason they do not choose Satan during the period of Jesus' reign is that Satan is not allowed any influence on earth.

Satan will deceive the nations no more. I want to finish with this very stern and serious word and I say it because I believe it to be true. What is Satan's main influence on earth? His greatest ministry is deception, and he can deceive Christians as well as unbelievers. Satan hates Revelation chapter 20 more than any other book in the Bible. Why does he loathe this chapter? Because it describes his end and his doom. The proof that he hates it is that he has deceived people outside and inside the church into believing that none of the words in Revelation 20 is true.

First of all, we have seen in this chapter that there will be a millennium —a reign of Christ for a thousand years on earth, before the earth passes away. The devil has not only persuaded people outside the church that there will be no such thing, he has also deceived many Christians into believing that there will not be such a thing. I meet good Christians who feel that there will be no reign of Christ on earth; the devil must be rubbing his hands in glee. I read that there are to be two resurrections; I read that there is a second death, and Satan hates that truth and he has deceived many Christians as well as unbelievers into believing that these things are not so. I read in this chapter that the devil is to be thrown into the lake of fire, and he has persuaded many people, including Christians, that there is no such place, and that hell is a naughty word that Victorian preachers used to frighten people and that it is not true and not real — and Satan rubs his hands. Consider these words: *They will be tormented day and night for ever and ever*. Nothing could be plainer; nobody could argue as to what that means, but the devil has persuaded even Christians to deny this truth and to stop believing that there could ever be such a thing as eternal punishment. You can see why Satan hates this chapter.

We learn from the next paragraph that there is to be a day of judgement when the whole human race will be divided into two parts only: those whose books of their lives tell their evil deeds, and those whose names are in the Lamb's book of life. There is no third possibility, and Satan has managed to deceive so many people into thinking that you make your heaven or hell here and that there is no heaven or hell hereafter, that there is no day of judgement, and that you cannot possibly divide the human race into two groups, the sheep and the goats. The devil must be laughing up his sleeve at us. Why does he deceive us into denying these things? Because he wants to drag as many down with him into that lake of fire as he can, that is why. He is determined to take the majority of the human race with him. Every Sunday when I get up to preach, he is determined to stop somebody listening. When I gave this series of talks on the book of Revelation there was one disturbance, one thing going wrong after another — to the building, to people, all kinds of things. There was something just before, or during, that sought to create a barrier between this truth and people. The devil would drag everyone down with him if he possibly could. So he hates this chapter and he will propose alternatives, conditional immortalities, second chance, purgatory —anything as an alternative to this. But here is the chapter in which the devil who appeared in the third chapter from the beginning of the Bible disappears in the third chapter from the end. The devil who came in to wreck and to ruin the human race, and who claimed the kingdoms of the world for his own, is to be utterly removed from the scene.

We should be thrilled that there is going to be no more evil, no more death, no more Satan, no more sin, no more darkness, no more sorrow, no more tears, none of the things that the devil has put in — all those words began in Genesis 3 — it is the vocabulary of Satan; but in Revelation 21 and 22 it is all over. Do not let the devil deny the truth in your mind of chapter 20 —Christ will reign, judgement will come, the human race will be divided, and there is a lake of fire. Do not let the devil rob you of those truths. Then, and only then, you will find that he cannot rob you of the joys and the assurance of glory and heaven. I have noticed that those who become less sure of hell also become less sure of heaven. Those who stop talking of the one tend to stop talking of the other. I remember reading an article in a national newspaper, by a reporter who had been asking people about life after death, and he wrote this way back in 1970: 'Forty years ago the British people stopped believing in hell, twenty years ago they stopped believing in heaven too.' You cannot pick and choose. We must have Jesus in all his majesty, Prophet, Priest and King, the Jesus who came to be our Saviour and the Jesus who comes again to be our Judge, the Jesus who is all of God, justice and mercy, pardon and punishment, *For in Christ all the fullness of the Deity lives in bodily form . . . .* It is this Jesus whom we welcome and praise. Let us cry 'hosanna' — save us now; blessed is he who comes.

The passage 20:11–15 is one of the shortest we have looked at from this wonderful book of Revelation, yet it is one of the biggest. The devil would love you not to believe that, if he could. He would do anything to stop you from thinking that one day every one of us will stand before God without our money, without our possessions, with nothing but a book in which is recorded everything that we have done. In this passage we see an amazing thing. Every*thing* has vanished and every*one* has come back. That is the vision that John now sees. The universe has gone, the earth has gone, the sky has gone, the sun has gone, the stars have gone, the moon has gone — and all that is left are people, and all the people who have ever lived are back again. Now this is a most amazing thing, it is exactly the opposite of what everybody else expects. Most people I talk to today expect every*body* to vanish before every*thing*. They expect the human race to bring about some dreadful atomic holocaust in which the race will perish, and many people believe that we shall commit racial suicide and leave a blank, bare earth covered in ash, radioactive dust, and an empty universe — that people will vanish and the universe will stay. The Bible teaches us that the exact opposite is true: the universe will vanish and all the people will come back. The heaven and earth had fled away — the only thing that is still there is a great white throne, but the rest has gone.

Then John looks and he sees all the people who have ever lived lined up before the throne. It is an incredible sight. Do you realise that one day you will see everybody who has ever lived back again when the earth has gone? *I saw the dead, great and small* —that means the important people and the insignificant people. Some people get the idea that the only people who last on are the famous people, the great people, the important people, but here we have everybody back again.

It is the scene of a courtroom but there are no witnesses —none is needed, God knows the whole truth. There is no jury —none is needed, because God is an impartial Judge. There are no advocates, either for the defence or for the prosecution —none is needed because God is truth. There are only prisoners in the dock and the Judge upon his seat. All who have ever lived — in the dock — and God upon the great white throne, that is the picture. It is made clear here that the entire human race will one day be divided into two groups and only two, and you will be in one or other of those two groups. There can be no escape, either from this day or from the division that takes place in it. On what basis are these two groups constituted? What is the dividing line that runs through every family, every congregation, every group of people on a bus, every group of people in a cinema? There is a line going right through them —what is that line? The line is discovered by opening certain books. Whether you treat these as literal books with paper pages or whether it is a metaphorical picture phrase, I care not. What it stands for is that there are records, and it is on the basis of the record that the division is made, and the first books to be opened are the books which record every man's life. In other words, somewhere in the universe is a book with your name on it, and everything that you have ever done is to be found in that book.

I do not know if you keep a diary. Perhaps you cannot be bothered —I cannot, except for appointments. Perhaps you write down a lot of things each day about what you have done. But, you know, your diary does not correspond to the book of which I am writing, because unless you are a very honest person there will be some things that you will never write down in the diary, some things that you would rather leave behind and forget.

The books are opened, and in these books is written everything that men have ever done. When the Bible talks about what you have done in your lifetime it includes what you have said, and what you have thought, and what you have felt. I wonder if you do not find that a most frightening thought, to be confronted with a book in which everything that you felt, and thought, and said, and have done in your brief lifetime on earth, has been recorded faithfully, accurately, honestly and impartially. It is a sobering thought because there is not a man or a woman who would be happy about facing that book — not one. We are only happy about our lives if we have managed by some trick of the memory to select from our past those things that we want to remember, but if we are honest there is not one of us who would like a film shown on a screen that showed everybody else what our thoughts have been even during the last week. There is no-one who would like me to play a tape recording of everything they have ever said, so that others could hear. But Jesus taught us that in this day, when the books are opened, what has been whispered in the bedchamber will be shouted from the house tops. Everything secret will be made open. The books will be opened for everybody to see. It is a sobering thought.

Let me clear up two misunderstandings. The first thing is that those books will not be account books with a kind of balance sheet on each page, with all the good deeds you did on the right-hand page and all the bad deeds on the left-hand page, with a double line and a kind of credit or debit balance at the bottom. You would be amazed at how many people think the books of God are kept like those of earthly accountants —they are not. God is not looking into the books to see if you did more good things than bad things, or bad things than good things, so that if you managed 51% good and 49% bad you are in, but if you managed 51% bad and 49% good you are out. Yet so many people think that a good day tomorrow cancels out the bad deed yesterday. It does not — all the deeds go down. And when a judge asks for the record of a man or a woman, he is not asking for the good record, he is asking: have they broken the law? The man who filled in the form at the Job Centre and answered the question, 'Have you ever been in prison?' with the word 'no', and then saw the next question 'Why?' and wrote, 'Never been found out', was at least honest. But the judge says, 'What is this man's record?' What he wants to know is how many other things he wants to be taken into consideration, how many other faults there have been. As far as the law is concerned it does not matter how many times you have kept it, the judge is concerned with whether you have broken it. In other words, if the policeman stops me for speeding and says, 'You were doing 45, we have got the radar trap at the top of the lane in the hedge', it is no use my saying to him, 'But officer, just consider, I stopped at the traffic lights at the top of the road, and indeed I stopped at the traffic lights further down, so that is twice that I have stopped at the traffic lights, and only once have I speeded, so surely . . . .' You try talking to the police like that! When God opens the books it is not to see if you have just managed to get enough good deeds to weigh it on that side, he is looking to see if you broke the law, and to break in one point is to break the law. Just suppose that you have broken God's laws only once a day. Supposing you have managed to keep it down to that, do you realise that if you have lived thirty years in full moral responsibility and age you will have to ask for ten thousand offences to be taken into account?

The second thing, to clear up misunderstanding, is this. God is a fair judge and will give us a fair trial, and he will not judge us for what we did not know to be wrong. The Bible makes that absolutely clear. Romans chapter 2 is the crucial passage if you want the actual proof. It is clear that he is only looking for your failure to live up to what you knew to be right. That is fair and just. This answers once and for all the problem: 'What about those who have never heard about Christ? What about those who have never heard of the ten commandments? What about those who do not know the laws of God?' Everyone has a conscience, and will be judged by his conscience as to whether his own conscience excuses or accuses him in that day. God will go through your life to see whether you lived up to what you *knew* to be right. Nothing could be fairer than that, and there is not a man or a woman in the whole world who would dare have that book open even on that basis.

I have talked to conceited people who have thought they were good. To people who have said, 'I am as good as so and so; I am as good as those who go to church', the one question they have not been able to answer is this: Have you lived up to what you knew to be right? Can you look me in the face and say, 'I have always followed the light as far as I could see it'? I have yet to meet somebody who could say yes. Which means, frankly, that on the basis of the books of our lives there is not one of us who can say anything other than 'Guilty, my Lord'

—not one. And since God is a God of justice, then he must carry straight through to the verdict and the sentence, and the sentence is the second death. The first death, which everybody has to go through, separates us from men and from earth; the second death separates us from God and from heaven. And it is the second death that I fear more than the first. It is the second death that men should be thinking about, not the first. The first is a separation that may be hard but at least it is not as final and terrible as the second — to be separated from God and from heaven.

Now let us look on the brighter side. There is another book that is opened on this day, and John sees it opened and it has one name on the cover — the name of Jesus. Across every other book is written the Judge's verdict of death, but across this book is written his verdict of life — it is Christ's book of life, it is the Lamb's book of life, and the simple fact is that out of all the millions who have ever lived there has been only one man whose life bears the most intimate scrutiny unscathed. There is only one life that you can examine every page, every word, every thought, every deed, every feeling and say, 'That man is perfect, that man has lived right, that man has lived straight; that man has lived pure' — and the man's name is Jesus. And he lived our life facing our temptations and our suffering and our death, and yet he lived right. Therefore across his book is written the word 'life'. But when that book is opened it will be seen to contain not only a record of his deeds, not only those miracles, not only the fact that he went about doing good all the time, you discover when you open that book that there are other names in it, and it is possible that there are names of people in your church who will be found in that book one day.

The Lamb's book of life contains more names than one, it

contains more than the name of Jesus, it contains the names of everyone who has believed in Jesus. Their name has been transferred from the book that had their own name on it to his book, and their name is in the Lamb's book of life. And the amazing thing is that in their book of their life there is nothing but blank pages —nothing written. Take this quite literally, that as soon as you believe in Jesus two things happen. The first is that everything wrong is blotted out from your book. That is a technical term that goes back to the day when they wrote on papyrus made of crossed reeds, pressed, and then given a shiny surface, rubbed and polished, and you wrote with a brush and ink on the papyrus. The words 'blotted out' mean to take a penknife, and with the blade scrape the surface off the papyrus, scraping the ink off with it, and then re-polishing so that it can be used again. You cannot really rub things out of today's paper as well as you could off papyrus. You could get it absolutely clean so that not even infra-red photography could find what had been written on it. And the word for 'blotted out' in the Bible is the word used for doing that to papyrus, paper. In other words, when I believe in Jesus, God takes his penknife and he just scrubs everything off out of my book, so that in the great day when the books are opened and the book labelled 'John David Pawson' is opened, it is full of blank pages. That is good news; that is the gospel; that is forgiveness. They will never again be brought up, and that is why I am a preacher of the gospel. To tell people that everything they have done that was wrong can be erased from the books of their lives is surely to bring good news.

The other thing that happens is that, while those pages are blotted out in the Lamb's book of life, a name is inscribed. When God opens that book it is the book of those who are acquitted in that day, the book of those who deserve life. How can a man who has done wrong be transferred from the one book to the other? How is that just? The answer is very simple. It is absolutely just because the day I believe in Jesus is the day that I recognise that my sins have already been paid for in the sight of the Judge, that atonement has already been made, that Christ died for my sins, for our sins, and not for ours only but for the sins of the whole world. Anybody who recognises that can get the record put straight in an instant. This is really just saying in another way John 3:16 — *For God so loved the world that he gave his one and only Son, that whoever believes in him shall not perish* [which is precisely what I would do if the book of my life was going to be opened] *but have eternal life* [which is what will happen when the Lamb's book of life is opened.]

This, then, is the revealing moment seen at the end of chapter 20. No-one will escape this moment, no-one can hide in a crowd, or even behind their family; each case is dealt with as an individual, each man is judged according to the books. And in that day it matters not whether you were important or insignificant, rich or poor. It does not matter then how many good deeds you did; it will matter terribly how often you broke the laws you knew to be true, and how often you fell short of what you knew to be right, but it will matter most of all if your name is in the Lamb's book of life. You will be in one or other of those two groups —there is no third possibility, and that is why we preach the gospel here, and that is why we are interested in missions, and preach the gospel throughout the world.

HOME AT LAST
Revelation 21 – 22

One meaning of the resurrection is this: it was the beginning of the new creation; and our Lord's body, raised from the dead — a body which has never died again, which has got no older, which has never been subject to suffering or hunger or thirst again — was the beginning of an entirely new creation, and the resurrection itself is the guarantee that God will one day re-create everything else, and that is why Jesus is called *the firstborn from among the dead.* So we are going to think about the new creation in chapters 21 and 22.

The only people who go through from chapter 20 to chapter 21 are those who belong to the Lord. Everybody else has gone. By the end of chapter 20 there is nothing left of the universe, and there is nothing left of the people in it, except God's people. The only beings from now on are God (the Father, the Son and the Holy Spirit) the angels in heaven, and God's people. But people need somewhere to live, and if you want to know the answer to the question 'What is meant by the phrase *going to heaven?*' you have got to read the last two chapters in the Bible. Almost everything we know about heaven is on these pages; there are a few hints elsewhere, but if we did not have the last two pages in the Bible we would know very little about heaven. As it is, we know a great deal.

There is a contrast between chapters 21 and 22 and the chapters immediately preceding, a contrast between an earthly city, Babylon, and a heavenly city, Jerusalem; between an earthly city that is likened to a prostitute and a heavenly city that is likened to a bride; between a dragon and a Lamb — and there is a great contrast between them; between an atmosphere of fear and weeping and one of joy and peace. The contrast is so marked that many people, alas, jump the earlier chapters straight into these because it is so wonderful to read.

There is not only a contrast between chapters 19 and 20 and chapters 21 and 22, there is a connection between the last two pages of the Bible and the first two — a remarkable connection; as big a connection as between the blind poet John Milton's two poems *Paradise Lost* and *Paradise Regained* — a tree of life that has disappeared and a tree of life that appears again; the disaster that befell the human race at the beginning of history, and the glory that awaits those who belong to God at the end of it. It is this connection between creation and re-creation which ties the whole Bible together and rounds it off beautifully.

We note that human language is being stretched to its limit here to describe the indescribable, and some have laughed at the picture language of pearly gates and golden streets. But why laugh? The language may be picture language, I do not know, but what I take from it is this: this is the most precious place there has ever been. It must be described in terms of the most precious things on earth, the costliest things and the most wonderful things —such as jewels and gold and transparent glass. These are the things that you have got to think of if you are going to begin to imagine a street in the city of the new Jerusalem.

Consider some basic questions. First of all, when does anybody see the new heaven? In the strictest sense it is not taught in the Bible that you go to heaven when you die — not heaven in the sense in which it is described here. This ought to be said. When we die, a Christian goes to be with the Lord. That is wonderful, better than anything here, but the Christian does not walk through the pearly gates into the golden streets when he dies. No-one will get there before anyone else; we shall get there together, we can explore it together, so we do not need to feel jealous of any who have got there first. This is something in the future. When does it all come? The answer is, when God has cleared away everything else. In other words, God has a kind of 'slum clearance programme' before he builds the city. He has to get rid of the universe as it is at the moment; he will remove all wickedness, all people who have chosen not to respond to his love. He will clear the site altogether, and then the new heaven and the new earth can come.

The first thing I want to emphasise very strongly indeed is this: there is to be a new *earth* as well as a new heaven. We must not think of heaven as some vague 'floating around' condition that has no tangible reality about it. The Bible does not just say there will be heaven; there will be a new universe. The word *heaven* refers to all that is not earth. The old heaven and the old earth are both terribly real, very tangible —those heavenly bodies that you see out in space on a clear night are just as real as your living room. What the Christian can look forward to is not floating around in a nightgown in some kind of vague cloudy place called heaven, but a new universe that involves a new earth as well as a new heaven, and we shall be able to move as freely from one to the other as Jesus did in his ascension.

It is very interesting to know what the new earth will be like. It will not be like this one, although it will probably be the same size. Think how much water there is, how much of the present earth is uninhabitable to men. We can cross it, we can go down under it in a submarine, but most of it is alien territory to us. We are told that the sea will be no more. Make the most of it, go to the seaside this summer! If you think you will miss it I can tell you that the new earth will be so wonderful, so much better than this one, that you will not even think about it — but it means that the whole earth will be available to man, as well as the whole of space. If you ever wondered what you would do in all eternity, exploring that universe would take quite a bit of your time — just wandering around God's wonderful creation. So there is to be a new heaven and a new earth — a new universe which is tangible, real. That is why we shall need new bodies, because it is all real; it is not something vague and spiritual, but rather something terribly physical, something utterly real, as real as the body of Jesus. When Jesus rose from the dead, he showed that he was not a ghost. The disciples could see and touch him; he cooked fish for their breakfast! He was the first born of all creation, and the new earth will be as real as the body of Jesus, and the new heaven will be, too.

Not only will there be a new creation, there will be a new communion between heaven and earth. At the moment there are great gaps in the universe which puny man is trying to cross, taking the first faltering steps. But heaven and earth come very close in these chapters, they link together. God and men come close, that is perhaps why. Instead of the sense that God is way up in heaven, here is a picture of God dwelling among men on earth. When Jesus came he was God visiting earth, but he only visited earth, and then he returned to heaven. Here we have a picture of God coming and *dwelling* with men and the word means staying with them — not just visiting. There is to be a new communion. To me, the most wonderful thing about heaven is this communion with God. The new heaven and the new earth will be fascinating, it will be wonderful to see all the people there, and to see those again that we have loved and lost in Christ, but to see God, to be with him, to live with him is in fact what makes heaven home. It is the Father's house; it is where you belong; it is where you stay.

Not only will there will be a new creation and a new communion, there will be a comfort for people. I suppose still the most lovely words in the book of Revelation, in a sense, are *He will wipe every tear from their eyes.* That phrase comes again and again in this book, and we are reminded of the way an earthly parent takes out a handkerchief and dries a child's eyes. This is what is going to happen there. At the moment God comforts us in our sorrow, in our death, in our troubles, in our suffering, and *in* all these things we become more than conquerors, but the comfort we are offered then is a comfort *out* of these things. Death is no more, sin is no more, suffering is no more. There will be no hospitals in heaven, no cemeteries in heaven, or in the new earth, so what a different place it will be. Life as we know it now is completely replaced by a new order of being —just as real as this, but far more wonderful.

Who will be there? Verses 5 – 8, are a kind of parenthesis which focuses our attention on the people involved in this new life, this new world. We have been looking at the new world, now we look at its inhabitants. The first person we are bidden to think about is God the Father himself. Do you notice that he so often begins his sentences with *'I'*. A man who does that is an egotist. Those who are constantly beginning their sentences with the little word 'I' are often self-centred. God alone can do this because God alone is completely selfless —God is love. And so he says: 'I make'; 'I am'; 'I give'. When you study the capital 'I' of the Bible you have got a study in itself, you could spend days just looking at the capital 'I's of God. *'I am making everything new!'* This will not be a patchwork universe with a bit patched up here, and a bit put right there, everything is new.

Not only that but, *'I am the Alpha and the Omega, the First and the Last, the Beginning and the End.'* He started it all off and he will finish it all. He sees a thing through. And: *'To him who is thirsty I will give to drink without cost from the spring of the water of life.'* Notice that a condition of knowing all this is that you are thirsty. Some people have no thirst for heaven. Some people would hate it, they really would, they have told me that if heaven is what the Christian thinks it is, then they would rather be in hell. I have had that said to my face. But to those who are thirsty, those who would love to have this kind of life, to them he will give. God is a God who says, *'I am', 'I make', 'I give'.* The trouble is that many people do not want all three, they want the *I give* bit, they are not sure about *I will make* and certainly they are not bothered about what *God is*, but these three belong together. Our interest is not just to be in what God gives to me but what God is in himself and what he is going to do —— that is a balanced interest in God.

So the Father will be there; who else will be there? The faithful will be there — those who have been faithful on earth to God, those who have conquered in the name of God, those who have put their faith in Jesus, now share this future. They have overcome and they now share. What we are here determines our future.

Who will not be there? We have a list of people who are absolutely forbidden to be there. It is very interesting that the list begins with the cowardly. Did you realise that cowardice is a sin, that cowardice is something that could keep you out of heaven? That is an astonishing statement; it is almost as startling as our Lord's teaching that worry is a sin. I relate it to something that Jesus said as often as he said anything else: *'Fear not.'* He said it in the same tone of voice as he said, *'Do not sin'*. It was a command because if you believe in God there is no need to fear.

The cowardly are followed up by the *unbelieving*, those who did not stay true, those who have not had faith in Jesus in their hearts. It is interesting that they are followed by *'the vile, the murderers, the sexually immoral'*. Now, note how God's lists of sins rarely correspond to human lists. The things that we would not put together, he puts together. He puts the cowardly and murderers together; a murderer does not usually have cowardice. We notice that murder is a sin not a sickness; we notice that the *sexually immoral* and *those who practise magic arts* and *idolaters* and plain *liars* are all lumped together: none of these people will ever get into glory —unless they are forgiven and have their names written in the Lamb's book of life. Verse 8 is the last mention of hell in the Bible. That kind of person joins the devil, the dictators and all the others.

Where is this new city? The angel of wrath now becomes the conductor of a tour of the new Jerusalem —a new task of mercy. When Jesus said, in John's Gospel, just before he died, *'I am going there to prepare a place for you'*, what do you really imagine he meant? Here we have a description. The place and the people who live in it are so identified with each other that the term *the bride* can be applied to both, because people live in community and the city is the bride of Christ because it is built for and inhabited by those who love him. So the holy city is given that wonderful description, the *bride* of Jesus, and indeed when John sees this city he can think of nothing else than a bride in all her glory, it is so like it.

Notice first of all that it comes down from heaven. It is not built up from earth like the tower of Babel, it is built down from heaven. It is not a human structure at all. While I like the music, I think the Women's Institute song, Blake's poem, is sheer rubbish — it is the most sentimental nonsense I think I have ever heard: 'And was Jerusalem builded here . . . ?'; 'And did those feet in ancient time . . . ?' The answer is: no, neither — and there is no point in singing about it, because it never happened. Jerusalem cannot be builded here, it has got to be built up there and it will come down complete. Let us sing about Jerusalem the golden, not Blake's poem. Let us face reality. The new Jerusalem is not something man can build among these 'dark satanic mills', it is something that must come down, full of light, out of glory, out of heaven.

Its magnificence is described first, it is dazzling, so dazzling that you almost have to screw your eyes up to look at it. No bride was ever so radiant. Its memorials are described. It is interesting that there are memorial names inscribed on the gates and the foundation stones, and when you look at them you discover that the memorials in this city are of the twelve tribes of Israel, the twelve apostles of the church. So the patriarchs and the apostles join together, the sons of Jacob and the disciples of Jesus. The twelve sons and the twelve apostles, all Jews. My naughty little mind wants to know whether Matthias or Paul is one of the twelve names. Judas will not be one of the twelve names and I am very interested to see which one is put in his place, but there are twelve apostles, twelve tribes of Israel — as much as to say that through all the history of the Jews and the Christians, Israel and the church, God was preparing the new Jerusalem. The future of the Jew and the Christian is inextricably bound up together.

The measurements of the city are quite startling. If you squared the moon off (just cut slices off to cube it) you would have the exact size of the new Jerusalem described here, which is a city cubed something like 1580 miles each way. So imagine a square in the sky, a city with broad piazzas or plazas (that is the very word used in the book of Revelation), with broad avenues, boulevards and squares, and with unimaginable buildings; and not just a flat town but a town that rises, a high-riser — a town that is cubed. Can you just imagine what it would be like to see that coming down out of heaven? It gets brighter and brighter, and as it gets nearer you see that it is just one city the size of the moon. The moon, of course, is a barren, desolate, dreadful place where men can hardly live, even though they take all the equipment with them. But that city is built for men to inhabit, a city where it will be glorious to live, and that is just the capital city of the universe, and the whole universe will belong to God's people. *'Blessed are the meek, for they will inherit the earth.'*

And so this city comes down out of heaven. Its size leaves one gasping; its materials are those of the most precious materials known to men. There are multi-coloured gates of single pearls. It is quite a thought that a pearl always results from injury and suffering. It begins when a little piece of grit gets inside the oyster, and to protect its soft flesh it secretes a hard coating to the grain of sand and builds that up. But the gates are made of pearls and the great street is pure gold. God's town planning. There will never be a town better planned than that one.

What about the conditions of life? We are told certain negative things that will not be there, and certain positive things that will be. The negative things: there will be no sanctuary.

Most cities have some religious symbol — it may be a spire or a dome or a tower, you often see against the skyline some religious object — but when you look round that city there will be no church to go to. You will not go to church there, you will be with God everywhere, all the time. These religious buildings are only religious props. There will be no sanctuary, no temple as there was in the old Jerusalem, the presence of God makes that unnecessary.

There will be no shadows. Oriental cities never sleep, and indeed the city of Babylon was a city noted for its nightlife —what went on in the dark. But here is a city of light, and there is no night there, no shadows, no street lamps, no moon, no stars, just brilliant light of God.

There will be no security, the gates will never be shut. There will be no need to, as there are no enemies, there is no danger, so why shut the gates? There will be no burglar alarms on anybody's house, there will be no danger, children will be able to play in the streets, people will be able to walk without fear down every street —think of that.

There will be no sin there, nothing unclean, nothing ungodly, nothing untrue — that means quite simply no rubbish dumps, no street cleaners, no dirt, a beautifully, perfectly clean city. We get excited about a stretch of clean air over a city, but our cities remain very dirty.

Finally, there is no suffering. The curse of God upon the human race has gone, there is nothing accursed, so there will be no suffering. The contrast is with the city of Babylon again.

Now let us turn to the positive side. It will be a cosmopolitan city. The kings of the earth will bring the wealth of the nations into it. There will be all nations there, every conceivable colour of people. It will be a healthy city, and the river and the tree by the river stand for this perfect health all the time. It will be a spiritual city; you will actually be able to see the face of the Lord. No man has seen God at any time, but when we get there we shall see what God looks like, and we shall have his name written on our foreheads, permanently belonging to him, stamped as people on earth had been stamped with the image of that earthly dictator (we saw the number, 666); here they will be stamped with God, belonging to God forever. The situation I have described will be permanent, *they will reign for ever and ever.* Hell is described as being for ever and ever, so is heaven.

This city will centre around the Father and the Son —God and the Lamb on the throne. It is Jesus' city because everybody in it is in his book of life, and his book of life corresponds to the roll of citizens there, with his throne at the centre.

We have come to the end of the book of Revelation and there is just a brief epilogue telling us what to do about it.

22:6

There are just five notes struck here to make a final chord in the symphony that we have been listening to. The first note struck is the note of inspiration. Who gave us this book? The answer is God himself with the same Spirit who inspired other prophets predicting the future. Therefore these words are absolutely trustworthy, you can trust every one of them to be true and to come true, for they are not just true they will *come* true. They are fact; every single thing that this book says will happen will certainly happen. Many of the things that this book describes you will read about in the newspapers, because newspapers will be produced until the end of the world, I presume; but many of these things you will never read in any other book or any newspaper.

To go through this book always lifts me out of the pettiness and the littleness of our human life into a larger realm where I get a bigger view of God and of the future. But what you must never do is to think too highly of the messenger who brings the message to you; you are not to think too highly of a preacher who preaches this book, or of John who wrote it, or of the angel who was the messenger to John. *Worship God!* It is the message that is important; who brings it does not matter. It is fellow servants — brethren, those who keep the words of the book — who bring it to you, but it is God's message. The inspiration of this book cannot be questioned. It has the divine stamp upon it. Verses 10–15 give us the incentive to do something about this book. The note of incentive is struck. The incentive is this: the challenge of the whole book is that everybody belongs to one category or another, of only two categories of people in the whole world — those who are filthy in God's sight and those who are righteous in God's sight; those who are evildoers in his sight, and those who are holy in his sight. There is no halfway house — you are either in one group or the other. This was typical of the teaching of Jesus, because when he had finished the Sermon on the Mount he said, *'For wide is the gate and broad is the road that leads to destruction, and many enter through it. But small is the gate and narrow the road that leads to life, and only a few find it.'* There is no other road. And the incentive to listen to this book is this: your future has been described in it. Either your future belongs with Babylon in chapters 19 and 20 or with Jerusalem in chapters 21 and 22. There is no other city mentioned — you are either caught up in the one or you will be caught up with the other — there is no alternative. Therefore, these verses divide people into the evil and the righteous, the filthy and the holy, and it is made clear that Christ is coming soon to deal with what every man has done. He is the Alpha and the Omega, the First and the Last, the Beginning and the End. Everything you can say of God you can say of Jesus, and it is he who will divide the sheep from the goats.

The third note struck in this chapter is a note of invitation: come, come, come. It is a note sounded by the Holy Spirit through the bride, which is the church; and by the Holy Spirit's indwelling, the church says come. Anyone who is thirsty can come and drink the water of life. It is a picture. It means: Do you seek real life? Do you seek the life that God can give you? Do you want life in him for evermore? Then, if you are thirsty, come and get it. Come, come — the word keeps repeating. It is the invitation from the Root and Offspring of David, that is Jesus — born of the holy line of David — the King. And it is the invitation from the bright Morning Star. There are 250 different names and titles of Jesus in the Bible, and here is the last, the bright Morning Star. What is that? It is the star that heralds the dawn. Did you see the dawn this morning? Did you see the morning star? Was the sky clear enough? That was the star that shines at the dawn of a new day, when the light is coming and the sun is going to burst out. Jesus is the bright Morning Star; he will still be shining at the dawn of this new day, and he says come.

The fourth note sounded in this final epilogue is a note of instruction, and it tells us a most solemn thing which I almost tremble to repeat, and it is this: if anyone adds anything to this book that is not in it then God will add plagues to them. There are sects and cults knocking at your door that have taken

247

this very book and added to it and found things in it which are not there, and it is their favourite book. There are even, alas, Christian teachers who put notes and headings right into this book, as if they can add to it and improve it in some way. Do not have a Bible with anything in it but the Word of God. You must not add to this book. You can seek to understand it, you can seek to talk about it to others, but do not add a word to it. And if somebody asks you a question about the future and God's prophecy does not give the answer then do not speculate, it is not good to do so. Do not add to what God has said about the future. People may say: Well, what about this, will we be doing this in heaven, or will we know that in heaven? The answer is that if God has not said anything about something, then I cannot tell you anything about it, and it is probably better for you not to know.

The second thing we are told that we must not do to the book of Revelation is subtract from it. That is the more common danger today, and I find many people who do it; I find so many people who love reading the last two chapters, and who know and can quote passages from the last two chapters, but who totally ignore the previous dozen chapters, and never read them, know nothing about them and could not quote anything from them, and could not talk to you about them. That is to subtract, it is to take away. You must take this book as a whole and as it stands. You must not be like the child licking the jam out of the sandwich, and lap up what it says about heaven and saying, 'But I can't accept what it says about hell' — lapping up what it says about Jesus saving people and helping them, but refusing what it says about Jesus destroying them. We must take the book of Revelation as it stands — all of it, no more, no less. We must not add anything to it, we must not

248

take anything from it. Somebody showed me a book that they had found in the public library called *Unfulfilled Prophecy*, a book by a woman gathering together predictions made by soothsayers and magicians and all kinds of horoscope readers right through the ages. Interestingly, I searched that book from cover to cover and there was not a single biblical prophecy mentioned — not one. This woman seems to have known every soothsayer, yet there was nothing from God's Word, and I was thankful there was not, because God's Word must not be mixed up with that kind of stuff. Do not read or study such stuff. Do not add to what God has said about the future, and do not take away from it.

Finally, there is a note of intercession. Three times in this chapter Christ mentions his coming again. And on all three occasions he says, *'I am coming soon'*. And so the intercession of the church is: *Amen. Come, Lord Jesus.* We want you, we want to see you, and we are longing and praying for the day, and you are welcome. So the book ends as it began. John, writing to the churches of Asia, said, *Grace and peace to you*; now he signs it off and says, *The grace of the Lord Jesus be with God's people*. Then comes the majestic word. The last word of the Old Testament is *curse* — *'. . . or else I will come and strike the land with a curse.'* The last word of the New Testament is *Amen*. [So shall it be. Amen.]

Lightning Source UK Ltd.
Milton Keynes UK
UKHW021124100720
366327UK00012B/1179